THE MATSYA PURANA

THE MATSYA PURĀNA:

A STUDY

BY

V. R. RAMACHANDRA DIKSHITAR, M.A.,
Lecturer in Indian History,
University of Madras.

UNIVERSITY OF MADRAS.
1935.

THE MATSYA PURANA

A STUDY

V. R. RAMACHANDRA DIKSHITAR

GYAN

Published by

Gyan Publishing House
5, Ansari Road
Daryaganj, New Delhi-110002
Phone: 011-47034999, 9811692060
E-mail: books@gyanbooks.com

Distribution Network
gyanbooks.com
India, USA, Canada, UK, Australia

ISBN: 978-93-7225-210-1 (HB)

First Published, 1935

2nd Impression 2025

Printed at: Gyan Press, Delhi.

THE MATSYA PURANA
Author: V. R. RAMACHANDRA DIKSHITAR

Bulletins of the Department of Indian History and Archaeology No. 5.

General Editor:

PROFESSOR K. A. NILAKANTA SASTRI

THE MATSYA PURANA

A STUDY

CHAPTER I.

FLOOD LEGENDS AND THE ORIGIN OF THE MATSYAPURĀṆA.

SECTION I.

FLOOD LEGENDS.

The origin and date of the Matsyapurāṇa have long been a matter of speculation among scholars. Orthodox tradition has it that this Purāṇa was revealed originally by Lord Viṣṇu in the form of a fish to Vaivasvata Manu, the first king of the solar dynasty who survived the deluge (Pralaya) which resulted in a partial dissolution of the world and not in its total annihilation. In this connection, two legends, the legend of the flood and the legend of the incarnation of Viṣṇu as fish require a careful investigation.

As the theory of incarnation of Viṣṇu as Matsya or fish is intimately bound up with the notion of a deluge, the Indian flood legends must claim our first attention. Next we shall examine other legend histories of the ancient world and see how far they are indebted to the Indian Flood legend. Lastly, we shall discuss how far these accounts of the flood are historical.

The Story of the Flood in Vedic Literature.

The earliest notice of the Indian Flood legend is found in the Vedic Literature—the Atharvaveda and the

Śatapatha Brāhmaṇa.[1] When Manu was washing his hands one morning, a fish came into his hands and said "Rear me, I will save thee from a flood which is going to devour all the creatures." It further directed him how to rear it. According to the direction Manu kept it in a jar. Finding that it outgrew that, he had a pond dug for it. The pond was found too small for its growing size, and it was hence taken to the sea. Then the fish advised Manu to prepare a ship and to enter into it when the flood came. The flood came, and Manu got into the ship and looked out for his saviour. The fish swam up to him, and to its horn he tied the ship when it passed to the Northern mountain. Here he fastened the ship to a tree. When the waters subsided, he descended from the mountain, afterwards known as " Manu's descent", from the *naubandhana* of the epic. Finding himself alone, Manu engaged himself in austerities. Being desirous of an off-spring he perfomed a pāka sacrifice and from the offerings a woman was produced. She was Iḍā, the daughter of Manu. Her Mitra and Varuṇa met. Through her, however, Manu generated his race and became rich in offspring and cattle.[2]

Now it will be interesting to see how this simple account of the flood grew in volume and extent as time rolled on. The epic Mahābhārata and the Purāṇas largely drew upon this old material of the Brāhmaṇa Literature and enlarged it and embellished it rather

1 I. viii, S.B.E., Vol. XII, p. 216 ff. Crooke: *Religion and Folklore of Northern India*, (1926), pp. 377-8; cp. Weber, *Ind. Stud.* I. pp. 161 ff. Max Muller, *History of Sanskrit Literature*, p 425 etc.

2 I have followed the translation of J. Eggeling.

unduly. Among the eighteen Mahāpurāṇas only four mention this legend and these are the Matsya, Bhāgavata, Padma and Bhaviṣya. It may be noted in the Bhaviṣya Purāṇa[3] that Noah of the Biblical account has been sanskritised as Nyūha. Without therefore taking into serious consideration the account in the Bhaviṣya Purāṇa, let us turn our attention to the account of the legend in the Matsya Purāṇa.

In the Matsya Purāṇa.

In ancient times Vaivasvata Manu abdicated his throne and was engaged in severe austerities to become the saviour of the world from the impending deluge. One day when he was offering a libation of water to the departed manes (*tarpaṇa*) a small fish fell into his hands along with the water.[4] In order to preserve this, the royal sage had it put into a water jar. But the fish grew so big that the jar could not hold it. Struggling for deliverance, it cried out to be saved. It was then thrown into a well. But its size soon grew to be more than what a well could accommodate. The king noticed this and took it to a pool of water, and then to the Ganges, and found that these, too, proved insufficient to accommodate the fish that was continually growing in size. Finally it was taken to the ocean. To the

3 III, I, 4, 47—57.

See for a comparative study of flood legends, Winternitz: Die Flutsagen des Altertums und der Naturvolker, (Mitteilungen der Anthropologreschen Gesellschaft in Wien, 1901,) p. 305—333. Th. Aufrecht refers to the Bhaviṣyapurāṇa as "ein literarischer Betrug." Z.M.D.G. (1903), Vol. 57, p. 276 ff.

4 Ch. I; see also MHB. IV. Ch. 187.

king's astonishment, the fish went on expanding until it filled the vast expanse of the sea. The King came to know that it was something more than an ordinary fish and prayed to God to let him know of its true nature. The fish soon showed itself to be Vāsudeva incarnate and addressed the king that, in view of the impending calamity of the deluge of the world, he had assumed the garb of a fish. Showing him the boat near by, Vāsudeva asked the king to rescue the distressed with the help of that boat, by tying it to its horn lest it should capsize. The deluge came and Manu did as he was directed. When the boat was floating in the dark waters, Vāsudeva, in the form of a fish, addressed the Matsya Purāṇa to Manu. We are reminded here of the legend of Oannes, the "Man Fish" quoted by Berosus.[5] It is said that 'Oannes swam up the Persian Gulf to the earliest Sumerian cities, Eridu and the rest, bringing with him the arts of civilisation', suggesting an early marine connection with a civilised land over sea.

In the Epic.

The same legend is briefly told in the Mahābhārata. In the Āraṇya Parva of the Mahābhārata, Mārkaṇḍeya, the sage, narrates the story of the Flood to Yudhiṣṭhira, the eldest of the Pāṇḍavas. According to it Manu Vaivasvata was a great rājarṣi, and after reigning over the kingdom as a true Kṣatriya, he took to the third āśrama, the Vānaprastha. In that stage he continued to perform severe austerities at a place called Badari. Once when engaged in performing

5 See Hall, *History of the Near East* (5th Ed.), p. 174, n. 2.

his daily duties on a river bank there came out a small carp from the water and appealed to Manu for succour. He put it in a small vessel. But when he found that it outgrew the size of the vessel, he took it successively to a well, a tank, the Ganges and finally to the sea. It grew larger and larger in its size. At that time the fish spoke to Manu of the coming flood and of the advisability of preparing a boat for saving himself with the seven sages (the saptarṣis) and all the seeds of life. The expected deluge came, and in the midst of the rolling waves the boat was tied to the horn of the fish and taken to the summit of the northern mountain, which came to be known as *naubandhana* from that day forward. Thus it was that Manu got the status of the creator of the living beings of the world.

In other Purāṇas.

This account of the epic bears intimate resemblance to that in the Matsyapurāṇa already noticed. In the latter version of the legend, instead of Badari, the Malaya hill is said to be the avenue where Manu Vaivasvata performed his penance. Otherwise the account agrees in details. The Bhāgavata account is still more complete and is inter-allied with the *avatār* of Viṣṇu. The purpose of this incarnation is said to be to recover the Vedas or revealed texts after slaying the demon Hayagrīva who had stolen them.[6] The names in this account are not Manu and Malaya. But it is Satyavrata, the royal sage, the king of Drāviḍa-deśa. This king was engaged in offering *tarpaṇa*

6 *Bhāgavata*. Trans. by S. Subba Rau, 1928, VIII, Ch. 24.

in the waters of the river Kṛtamālā when the fish is said to have crept in. What follows is common to all the versions. But here the god fish informs him that he would become the Vaivasvata Manu after the deluge, and that a Manvantara would then begin after his name.[7] This shows that while the Bhāgavata, the Padma and the Agni follow a certain tradition, the Matsya Purāṇa follows the epic tradition which is more ancient and much more authentic.

The Chaldean account.

Before we proceed further to examine the other aspects of the Indian flood legend it would be interesting to know something of the other accounts like the Chaldean and the Jewish. The account of the Chaldean flood was furnished by Berossos (also Berosus), a Babylonian priest and a contemporary of Alexander the Great. He wrote a history of Babylon in Greek. The full work is not now available. But fragments of it carefully preserved by later Greek historians, just like those of Megasthanes on India, throw welcome light on the history of ancient Babylon. Curiously the Berosusian account of the flood is corroborated by the history of Gilgamish, recovered from the long lost archives of Assyria. It is a poem in twelve tablets which records the heroic exploits of an ancient king of Erech.[8] The eleventh canto is devoted to the story of

7 This version is repeated in the Agnipurāṇa (Ch. 2, 3—17) and the Padmapurāṇa with slight variations (VI, 258, 11—31).

8 See Wallis Budge, *the Babylonian story of the Deluge*, p. 25.

the flood. It is said that Xisuthrus[9] the last of a dynasty of ten kings was the Hero of the Flood. To him in a vision the deity Kronus appeared and informed him of the coming Flood. The deity enjoined him to build a vessel and to take with him his wife, friends and relations besides different species of birds and animals after burying the sacred scriptures in the city of the Sun at Sippara. Xisuthrus did as he was commanded to do. The flood came and subsided. He found himself entangled in the mountains of Kurdistan in Armenia. He got tested the abatement of waters on the surface of the earth by letting birds fly thrice. Then he got out of the ship and offered sacrifices to the gods. By his piety he was translated to the realm of gods, as also his wife and daughter with the pilot. Others in the vessel journeyed towards Babylonia.[10]

There is again epigraphic evidence testifying to the antiquity of the Babylonian flood legend.[11] In the course of excavations undertaken by the Turkish Government at the site where the ancient city of Sippara stood, there came to light a broken tablet dated the 28th day of the eleventh month in the eleventh year of the King Annirzaduga roughly B. C. 1966. It contains references, though mutilated, to the flood story of Babylonia. To these versions in the Semitic language, comes another fragment of a tablet discovered at Nippur in the exacavations conducted by the University

9 The name Xisuthrus answers to the cuneiform Si-sit or Tsisit, apparently a Greek corruption of the name on the tablet Khasisadra. See Cory, *Ancient Fragments*, pp. 48—49 (London, 1876).

10 *Ibid*: pp. 60—63.

11 See Winternitz, *op. cit.*, p. 32.

of Pennsylvania, but inscribed in the Sumerian script, containing a tradition of a great deluge, assigned approximately to 2100 B. C. This date is significant, for, by this time in the third millennium before the Christian era, the Sumerians had become absorbed in the Semitic population and had almost ceased to exist as a distinct race. And it is generally accepted that the Babylonians borrowed the story of the Flood from the Sumerians and therefore this legend must be of considerable antiquity.

The Hebrew Accounts.

Before we finally state the probable source to which the Sumerians themselves were indebted, it is of considerable interest to examine the Hebrew account in the Genesis, for this reason, viz.: that there is an agreement between the two versions, the Sumerian and the Hebrew. In both of them the two events, the creation of man and the Deluge, are intimately connected with each other. The other point of concord is in the view both take the creation of man as antecedent to the creation of animals.

The striking resemblances in essential features between the Babylonian and the Sumerian, between the Sumerian and the Hebrew stories of the great flood, compel us to pass on to an examination of the Biblical flood legend. This is commonly known as the Hebrew Flood. Biblical critics, who have examined the legend as recorded in the Book of Genesis,[12] detect

12 See Frazer, *Folklore in the Old Testament*, pp. 56—7.

two versions of the same story apparently not consistent with each other, the one derived from the Priestly Code and the other from the Jehovistic Document. Of these the document of Jehovah is held to be earlier in date than the Priestly Code. It is said that there are material differences between the accounts of these two documents in respect of animals clean and unclean, the duration of the flood, causes alleged for the flood, etc. But we are not concerned here with such details. Coming to the Great Flood, Noah is the hero of this Legend. A descendant of Adam and Eve, Noah led a pure and clean life. The world became full of evil, and wickedness increased all round. The Lord, who was a friend of Noah, communicated to him his resolution to destroy the world by unprecedented floods, and advised him to escape in an ark of gopherwood with family, two fowls among the many and seven of the beasts. There was a continuous downpour of rain for forty days and nights and the consequent floods did not subside for 150 days. After that long period, it is said, that land was discovered by letting a raven and a dove to fly. The ark was found stranded on Mount Ararat. The story is thus concluded, viz.: that Noah brought forth three sons, Shem, Ham and Japheth who were the progenitors of human beings on earth.[12a]

Flood legends of other ancient countries.

It is a fact universally recognised that primitive religion and science alike indulge more in what

12a Genesis, VI—VIII.

Sir Edward Tylor has called "myths of observation" rather than historical tradition. Facts of physical geography were ascribed by early writers on religion, to some great primeval cataclysm or tremendous catastrophe as a result of some divine agency at work. In this way we have to understand many of these world myths. So have risen the great stories of a great flood, Thessaly being one of the early seats of the legend. Literature and tradition of ancient Greece place on record three kinds of Flood which the world had witnessed at different times. These were in the epoch of the Ogyges, King of Thebes in Boeotia, of Deucalion and his wife Pyrrha, and during the epoch of Dardanus, better known as the flood of Samothracian tradition. Aristotle and Plato refer to the deluge in Deucalion's time, and according to the chronological table drawn up by the Parian chronicler in 265 B. C. this deluge is said to be dated in the year 1539 B. C. It is said that there was an earthquake between Mount Ossa and Olympus arresting the natural course of the river, Peneus, resulting in the inundation of its waters, producing a flood over the land. The date of its occurrence is approximately fixed 1503 B. C.[13] According to the latest researches the opening of the Bosphorous, which deviated the water of the Aralo-Caspian Sea flow into the European Mediterranean, must have been an occasion of an inundation of the low lying coasts of Asia Minor, Africa, and Greece facing the Mediterranean. If this inundation could be taken to have occurred in the reign of Deucalion about 1503 B. C., the Aralo-Caspian

13 Lemprière's *Classical Dictionary*, p. 200.

Sea, which extended as far as the Black Sea, must have disappeared in early historical times. In the light of this fact the theory of Central Asia as the original home of the Aryans[14] cannot gain support as that sea-covered region would not yield enough pasturage to a pastoral people as the ancient Aryans were. We refer to this cataclysm as there are substantial resemblances between the Greek stories and the Babylonian version of the catastrophe.

These are not all. The traditionary lore of every country in the world has some version or other of a great Flood. There are the flood legends of Ancient Egypt where Tem is said to be the father of all mankind. Similar stories of a cataclysm here, or of a catastrophe there, are found in the literature of primitive folks throughout the world. Sir J. G. Frazer, to whose learned work we have referred even at the outset, examines interesting particulars of stories of a great flood in Eastern Asia, in the Indian Archipelago, in Australia, in New Guinea, and Melanesia, in Polynesia and Micronesia, in South America, in Central America and Mexico, in North America and in Africa, and the reader who is interested in details is referred to that authority.[15]

Causes of diluvial traditions.

A critical inquiry into the different versions of the flood legend leads us to infer that these diluvial tradi-

14 A. C. Das, *Rig Vedic India*, p. 39—40.

15 J. G. Frazer: *Folklore in the Old Testament*, Ch. IV.

tions are the consequence of three factors; inundation of the sea, heavy and continuous downpour of rain, and earthquakes. Modern history furnishes examples of such inundations of the earth by the rising tides or of devastation by rain and earthquakes. A specific instance which is still green in our memory is the havoc caused by the earth tremor recently in Behar. It is recorded, according to the Scientific Indian, that an earthquake at the mouth of the Indus (1810) resulted in forming a lake covering 2000 square miles. If this were so now we may imagine similar occurrences in days of antiquity also. Modern geological researches lend support to the theory of occurrences of floods and devastation of the land by the erosion of the sea as in Western Asia, Southern India and other parts of the world. Oldham says: "At the close of the cretaceous period and some time before the commencement of the tertiary era the great Indo-African continent was finally broken up and all but the remnants in India and South Africa sunk finally beneath the Sea.'[16] 'Again: 'The present Western coast of India and the elevating of the Western Ghats begin from the middle of the tertiary epoch or a little earlier'.[17] In the light of these known facts it is not hazardous to confirm the conclusion that these versions of a flood are after all reminiscenses of actual facts, though some of them may be partly legendry and partly mythical. That these diluvial legends are then based on historical traditions cannot be gainsaid except in the few cases which may be only myths of observation.

16 *Geology of India*, p. 494.

17 *Ibid.* p. 49.

They do not deserve to be summarily dismissed as the mere imagination of the fertile brain of a poet or a priestly writer. But the real difficulty presents itself when we try to locate the origin of these stories. Is there any identity of origin, or does every account stand by itself? Or again is a floating tradition engrafted upon a native legend? Differences of opinion exist, and it is for future research to decide one way or the other.

Mutual indebtedness.

Recent archaeological discoveries have revealed to us a new vista of an ancient and wonderful civilization in the Indus region the age of which has been assigned to the chalcolithic period. There is sufficient testimony to the view that the Indus people must have migrated to Elam, Tunis, Babylon, and even to Egypt.[18] None will at least deny the cultural contact between these countries in this ancient period. Utilising to the full the whole volume of these memorials, literary and archaeological, there can hardly be two opinions that the migration of the culture must have been from the Indian Home rather than the other way about. Among others the following may be cited as evidences: First, the cults of Śiva and Śakti and the practice of Yoga are all distinctly Indian in character, adapted by the legends of Elam, Sumer and other countries. The finds of female statutes like the figures of Mother Goddess in several places in Western Asia, the sacred Tree of Life in Babylonia, and the Sumerian God Enkidu, bear

18 See my article on the *Culture of the Indus Valley*, where I have discussed this point. *Journ. of Mad. University*, Jan. 1934.

testimony. Secondly, there is the evidence of pottery. The Sumerians took with them the Indian Potter's arts from Sind. Unlike in India the painted pottery died out very early in both Mesopotamia and Sumeria.[19] If this assumption of migration from India be correct one has to venture a conjecture that the Vedic legend as seen in the Śatapatha Brāhmaṇa was the parent of other flood legends,[20] and as there was active intercourse between India and Babylon and Egypt,[21] it is natural that these legends caught the fancy of the ancient peoples who adopted it as a convenient framework for tracing the origin of human race after a periodical destruction of the world or a part of the world by floods of unprecedented character. For, according to the Hindu literary tradition, it was only a partial deluge and not a mahāpralaya which enveloped all the worlds including those above at one sweep. Thus the Hebrew version had the Babylonian for its basis, the Babylonian the Sumerian and the Sumerian the Indian version.

Frazer's Criticism.

Commenting on the form of the story as it is narrated in the Śatapatha Brāhmaṇa Frazer remarks: "Nothing whatever is said about rescuing his wife and children. The omission betrays a lack not only of

19 *Ibid.*

20 See Prof. A. S. Vaidyanatha Aiyar's article in J.B.H.S. II, pp. 1—14, cp. Frazer, Ch. IV, *Folklore in the Old Testament*, (Macmillan, 1923.)

21 See the leading article of Prof. H. Frankfort in the Annual Bibliography of the Kern Institute (1932).

domestic affection but of common prudence on the part of the philosopher, and contrasts forcibly with the practical foresight of his Babylonian counterpart, who, under the like distressing circumstances, has at least the consolation of being surrounded by the family circle on the stormy waters and of knowing that as soon as the flood has subsided, he will be able with their assistance to provide for the continuance of the human race by the ordinary process of nature. In this curious difference between the two tales is it fanciful to detect the contrast between the worldly prudence of the Semitic mind and the dreamy asceticism of the Indian?"[22] If we take into account the circumstances under which Manu became the originator of this race, then this charge of lack of domestic affection against Manu can not be levelled. Manu, the king, had relinquished the world and had entered into austerities in a spirit of renunciation and detachment when the great flood occurred. Domestic affection means that one is a worldly man, materialistic in his outlook: and the spirit of attachment, which is a thorn in the path of release from the circle of births and deaths, will be the prevailing factor. When the catastrophe occurred, Manu was a sage, and as a sage he had neither family nor affection. Therefore it is unfair to charge him with lack of worldly prudence. On the other hand that he had this in full is seen from the fact that after the flood he created a woman, and through her became the father of the human race. Judging by the form of the story itself in the Śatapatha Brāhmaṇa one will not be far wrong to infer

22 Frazer, *op. cit.*, p. 134.

that it is the oldest version which has been improved upon by its borrowers according as their fancy led them. As we have already said, while the flood is caused in some countries as a result of volcanic eruptions and earthquakes, in other countries it is due to heavy downpour of rains or erosion of the sea.

The probable date of the flood.

Now comes the profoundly interesting speculation as to the date of this Flood. The question is whether there are enough materials to make at least an approximate conjecture. This is not impossible if we are prepared to revise our chronological estimate of the Vedic literature. On the basis of the astronomical facts yielded by the passage: एतान् हवै कृत्तिकाः प्राच्यै दिशे नच्यवन्ते in the Śatapatha Brāhmaṇa, S. B. Dixit has fixed the date of this work at 3000 B. C.[23] This may or may not be acceptable. But if the said astronomical data could be pressed into service, and if the Ṛg Veda Samhitā can be taken to an epoch preceding the Chalcolithic period of the Indus culture, we can arrive at a tentative conclusion. For, it is significant that the Ṛg Veda Samhitā is silent in respect of the Flood though it refers to the seismic disturbances in the Saptasindhu. From the absence of any reference to the Flood it would be logical to conclude that the Flood was still a thing of the future. The mention in the Śatapatha Brāhmaṇa shows that the Flood had become a thing of the past. Hence a milestone may be fixed between the epoch of the Ṛg Veda Samhitā and that of the Śatapatha Brāhmaṇa.

23 See the *Indian Historical Quarterly*, 1933, p. 923.

The Place of the Flood.

According to the Matsya Purāṇa the place where Manu, the hero eponymos of the Vedic mythology and son of Āditya Vivasvat, performed his penance, is the Malaya Hill in South India. This receives further corroboration from the Bhāgavata Purāṇa where reference is made to the king of the Drāviḍadeśa in connection with the Deluge.[24] This theory gains further support, if the five tribes of the Ṛg Veda,[25] who are supposed to be the offspring of Father Manu, bear any affinity to the five natural geographical divisions of the territory to which the Tamil Śangam Literature makes such pointed reference. The geographical divisions of people, according to Tamil literature are maritime, hilly, sandy, agricultural and forest.[26]

Added to this are the geological and other evidences. A number of human relics, preserved among the gravels of the rivers Godāvarī and Narmadā as well as in other alluvial areas of South India, testify to man's existence in prehistoric times. Whether man existed in an age earlier than the older alluvia of the Godāvarī and the Narbadā, and whether he was a witness of nature's last great phenomenon, viz., the erection of the Himalayan chain to its present height,

24 Drāviḍadeśa in ancient Indian Literature means only Tamiḷagam, and does not include Andhra, Karnāṭaka and Mahārāṣṭra as the late Dr. Caldwell would have it.

25 Ṛg Veda, III, 24—3.

26 For a full account see my '*Studies in Tamil Literature and History*, p. 274.

are moot questions for students of Indian anthropology.[27] If anthropology will bear testimony to the existence of man in this part of India in much earlier times than the older alluvia of the Godāvarī and Narbadā, this will tend to confirm the literary evidence furnished by two of the Mahāpurāṇas.

From these circumstantial evidences of the Purāṇa and allied literature we have to infer that there was not one Deluge but several deluges which occurred from time to time. In the same way as the incarnation of the Matsya or fish is connected with the deluge, the incarnations of Tortoise (Kūrma) and of Boar (Vārāha) are also connected with deluges.[28] Hence the Purāṇa is clear when it mentions a partial deluge as different from a full deluge. This must have occurred in different countries at different periods of the prehistorical and protohistorical epochs. But the striking similarity of these different versions indicates that these accounts migrated from one part of the world to another. This was indeed a characteristic feature of ancient folklore.[29]

Coincidences between Babylonian and Indian Legends.

As has been already said, in the epoch when Alexander lived there was one Berosus who wrote the

27 Wadia, pp. 269—270.

28 See *Śat. Br.* VII, 5, 1—5; *Tait. Samh.* VII, 1, 5—1; See Muir, *Original Texts*, I, pp. 52 and 54.

29 See my paper on '*The Migration of Legends*' in the *Annals of Bhandarkar Institute*, Vol. XV, pp. 212—19.

history of the Chaldeans and other treatises, fragments of which have been unearthed. The first book is devoted to the history of Babylonia. Here Berosus informs us "that there were written accounts preserved at Babylon with the greatest care, comprehending a term of fifteen myriads of years. These writings contained a history of the heavens and the sea; of the birth of mankind; also of those who had sovereign rule; and of the actions achieved by them".[30] Without stretching the imagination too far we can say that these documents are quite analogous to the Hindu Purāṇa Literature which are traditionally divided into five similar topics named Pañcalakṣaṇa. Does this not suggest migration of legends and literature from Ancient India to Babylon? Possibly it does.[31]

SECTION II.

THE ORIGIN OF THE PURĀṆA.

The Matsyas in the Vedic period.

The origin of the Matsya Purāṇa is far from being settled. It cannot be that the extant Matsya Purāṇa can be referred to a period when the Father of all mankind was born. In giving an account of its own origin it is said to be the revelation of God fish to the Father of all mankind during the course of the Deluge. Nor are the style and language archaic and ancient to warrant even such an assumption. So we venture to

30 Cory's *Ancient Fragments*, p. 56.

31 For another view, see Rawlinson, *Intercourse between India and W. World*, p. 15.

think that the kernel of the account is to be traced to the ancient tribes who went by the name of the Matsyas. Their ancientness is seen from a passage of the Ṛg Veda[32] where they figure among the enemies of Sudas. Next in the Śatapatha Brāhmaṇa, a Matsya King is mentioned by name Dhvasan Dvaitavana.[33] Thus it is evident that the Matsya tribe was a very ancient tribe, enjoying the status of an independent kingdom from the epoch of the Ṛg Veda Samhitā.[34] We hear, again, in post-Vedic Indian Literature, of the Matsya country, and tribes known as the Matsyas as the inhabitants of the Matsya country. Manu would include this in the Brahmarṣideśa.[35] The identification of this country will be valued by a student of the historical geography of ancient India. The Matsya kingdom seems to have been covered by the modern Dinajpur, Rangpur and Cooch Behar. Two divisions of the Matsya country are, however, distinguished. While one of these is identified with Jaipur, the other must be placed farther to the West, or in Guzerat.[36] The latest researches of Nundo L. Dey have gone a long way to confirm these results. The Matsya deśa, he says, comprised the territory covered now by Jaipur and included the whole of the present territory of Alwar with a portion of Bharatpur. In the epic age,

32 VII, 18—6.

33 XIII, 5—4—9.

34 *Vedic Index*, II, p. 121.

35 II, 19, VII, 193.

36 See p. 390 of Garret's *Classical Dictionary*, Madras, 1871. See Bandarkar, *Carmichael Lectures*, (1918), pp. 52—3. *The Geographical Dictionary* (Luzac, 1927, pp. 128—9).

however, it was largely the kingdom of king Virāṭa where the Pāṇḍavas resided incognito during the last year of their exile. In the Buddhist literature Maccha or the Matsya deśa figures as one among the sixteen mahājanapadas or kingdoms.[37] It appears that part of South India was sometimes identified with the Matsya deśa. There is, first, the statement of the Matsya Purāṇa that the fish appeared to Manu performing austerities on the Malaya Hills.[38] Next light comes from another quarter as if to corroborate this theory. We have a lake by name Matsya-tīrtha not far from the river Tungabhadrā in the Mysore State full of fishes producing musical sounds reminding us of the singing fishes called Butterman off the coasts of Scotland, or of Ceylon.[38a]

Not altogether unrelated to the subject is the reference by Huien Tsiang[39] to the legend of the Vajjian Fish monster in days long past with 18 heads, each with two eyes, which was instructed by the Tathāgata who came to the riverside, the residence of fishermen. It is said that the fish was a Brahman in the previous birth who reviled the Buddhas and ridiculed the priests. Hence it was born as a fish with a monstrous body. This legend refers to an area which is apparently the eastern Matsya deśa comprising the south portion of Tirhut including Vaiśāli.

37 Cp. S.B.E., XVII, p. 146 n.

38 Ch. I.

38a See N. L. Dey—*The Geographical Dictionary*, (Luzac, 1927), p. 129.

39 Beal, *Records of the Western World*, II, p. 78 ff. cp. *Mahābhārata*, Sabhā Parva, Ch. 30.

Other evidences for identification.

There is a tradition to show that once South India of the extreme south was known to be Matsyadeśa. According to the Kāvēri Purāṇa or Kāvēri Mahātmya of the Skānda Purāṇa, the country to the north of Malabar and to the West of Rāmanāthpura (Hassan Dt.) and six leagues to the east of the Western Ocean went by the name of Matsyadeśa. It is said that in a holy spring near the Ardhacandra mountain (probably Candragutti in Shimoga district), Viṣṇu took the form of a fish and worshipped Śiva. This country is now covered by the major portion of modern Coorg.[40]

That the Matsya kingdom continued to outlive many other ancient Indian kingdoms is evident (see Huien Tsiang's reference). In the time of Dharmapāla of the Pāla dynasty and after A. D. 800 there is the record of two grants which bear witness to the installation of Cakrāyudha in the Pāñcāla capital of Kanauj by Dharmapāla with the assent of the neighbouring powers, enumerated as the Bhoja, Matsya, Madra, Kuru, Yadu, Yavana, Avanti, Gandhara and Kira kings.[41]

This is not all. The South Indian inscriptions often mention the Matsya family chiefs in Orissa. These chiefs seem to have had some status in the Ganjam and Vizagapatam districts which went once by

40 For this tradition and other details connected with it, see Lewis Rice, Mysore, III, pp. 85 seq. and esp., pp. 89—91

41 Smith, Early History of India, p. 418.

the name of Matsyadeśa. A list of six kings is given commencing with Arjuna A. D. 1269 and ending with Jayanta alias Śri Kṛṣṇavardhana 1339.[42] The Dibbidda grant[43] gives the full geneology of the line and makes Arjuna the 23rd in descent from Ganga the founder.[44] But from the materials available one cannot say whether these chiefs had any connection with the earlier Matsyas though it seem's reasonable to take them as a branch of the ancient Matsya dynasty. We hear that the Madagole Zamindars of Vizagapatam claim to have been descended from a fish. Their throne is fish-shaped, and on their banner figures a fish.[45]

South India, the original place of the Purāṇa.

Thus we see that branches of ancient Matsya family spread over all parts of India. These ancient tribes had probably the totem of fish and cultivated the fish legend of old. It is quite possible that the Matsya Purāṇa originally started with the Matsya tribe, and like other legends of Hindu mythology began to travel throughout the ancient Indian continent. It would appear that the floating legend was reduced to writing for the first tim'e in South India. In support of this theory the following evidences may be cited. While most of the Mahāpurāṇas do scant justice in their

42 See for this list, Sewell, Historical Inscriptions of South India, p. 366.

43 51 of the inscriptions of the Madras Presidency, by V. Rangacarya, Vol. III, p. 1673.

44 See also *Ep. Ind.*, Vol. V, p. 106—12.

45 See *Man in India*, Vol. XII, April, 1932, p. 96.

reference to South India, the Matsya Purāṇa is full of it. The compiler's knowledge of Dekhan and South India is fairly accurate. We have the names of Elāpuram, Rāmeśvaram, Tāmraparṇi, Śrīraṅgam, Ekāmbhakam, and Āmrāteśvaram and references to well known hills like the Malaya mountains, and Tiruccengode hill (Salem District), which alone answers to the description of the Purāṇa of an Ardhanārīśvara temple with a Viṣṇu shrine in its compound. Details of similar geographical data seem to point out to the fact that the Purāṇa might have originated in South India. Two other characteristically South Indian features are the place of honour given to the moon God as an independent deity much celebrated as such in the early Tamil Śangam Literature,[46] and the mention and use of betel leaves[47] first introduced in South India from Java and then spread to the other parts of India.

SECTION III.

THEORY OF INCARNATION.

This section is devoted to an examination of the theory of incarnation of which the Hindu sacred texts tell us so much. It is usual to speak of the daśāvatāram or the well known ten incarnations of Lord Viṣṇu. These are Matsya (fish), Kūrma (tortoise), Vārāha (boar), Narasimha (half-lion and half-man), Vāmana

46 See my article *Lunar Cult in India, Ind. Ant.*, 1933.

47 Ch. 215, 15.

(the short man), Paraśurāma, Rāma, Kṛṣṇa, Buddha, and Kalki. Though this is the accepted tradition of the ten avatārs,[48] there is another version of these avatārs in the Matsya Purāṇa. Twelve avatārs are mentioned there as being incarnations of Viṣṇu during the twelve battles between the Devas and the Asuras to relieve the former from their distress.[49]

The fish and the Record of the rocks.

The second version which is slightly different from the first shows that there is no unanimity in tradition. Similarly, we have seen that there were as many as 28 avatārs of Maheśvara mentioned in the Vāyu Purāṇa.[50] But of these the theory of Daśāvatār is interesting, and to a student of ancient history, the Hindu theory suggests the idea of evolutionary process of human development.[51] In the story of the development of the human race, we see that life is not stable but shows a tendency to change continually though slowly. H. G. Wells remarks :

48 See Kṣemendra's *Daśāvatāracaritra* (Kāvyamāla No. 26, Bombay, 1891). It may be noted in passing that these devices and others of Hindu Mythology were used on the coins issued by the Hindu rulers. For example, these devices are seen in the coins of the Vijayanagar Empire. See Ar. Sur. of Mysore, 1929, pp. 30—31. See also T. A. Gopinatha Rao—*Elements of Hindu Iconography*, Vol. I, Pt. 1, 119 ff.

49 Ch. 47, st. 41—45.

50 Vāyu, Ch. 23.

51 We are told by Pancanan Mitra of the Calcutta University in his *Prehistoric India*, (II. Ed., 1927), that an eminent Bengali thinker elaborates in a Bengali work the idea of incarnations indicating the stages of spiritual progress revealed at various times in the earth, the last being yet to come, p. 428.

"Wherever the shore line ran there was life, and that life went on, in, and by and with water as its home, its medium, and its fundamental necessity. The first jelly-like beginnings of life must have perished whenever they got out of the water, as jelly-fish dry up and perish in our beaches today."[52] We know life needs air and light. It equally needs water to drink and digest the food taken. The record of the rocks or the science of geology furnishes us with the fact that out of the Early Palaeozoic Seas, emerges the fish, the first of the vertebrate series.

Traditional origin of the earth and vegetation.

This receives corroboration from the Vedic and the post-Vedic literature of the ancient Hindus. The Ṛgveda Samhitā speaks of a state of non-existence,[53] and of the origin of vegetation (oṣadhi) in a period removed by three yugas from the epoch of the devas or Gods.[54] When the Vāyu Purāṇa[55] states that the earth was originally a mass of fire and was replaced by water, it restates the idea of the Taittirīya Samhitā[56] that originally everything was in a liquid state which was in time transformed into the Dyau and Pṛthvī.[57] A case has been made out that the "Dyau" was another country like the earth on

52 The *Outlines of History*, p. 30, (5th Ed.).

53 X. 72:2.

54 *Ibid.*, 97.

55 VI. 1.

56 VII, 1, 5:1.

57 *Cp.* R.V. X, 81:1.

the surface of the globe, and was not a reference to sky as is generally accepted.[58] It is contended that 'Dyau' was the first to become dry land, and from the terms *pita* or *janita* in the Ṛgveda Samhitā appended to the 'Dyau',[59] it is argued that it was the fatherland where fire was first kindled,[60] and consequently the earth became the motherland. Taken by itself the evidence is hardly sufficient to establish so important a conclusion. Then it is said that Indra made the earth terra firma as also the mountains.[61] Next came a series of what we may call the geological life types,[62] the herbs on earth,[63] and the fish[64] or tortoise,[65] and the man-lion,[66] and lastly the Dwarfman.[67]

Aṇḍaja and Jarāyuja.

Aeons pass by. The next stage in the evolution of the living species is reached when the amphibians (aṇḍaja) lay their eggs in and under water. The tadpole stage of the later Palaeozoic gives place to reptiles, which took their origin from certain amphibians which had acquired reptilian characters.

58 See *Sarasvati Bhavana Studies*, Vol. IV, (Benares, 1925), p. 174.

59 *Ṛgveda Samhita*, IV, 1:10; VI. 70:6, etc.

60 *Ibid.*, X. 45. 8 etc.

61 *Ibid.*, II, 12:2.

62 *Taitt. Up.* II. 1.

63 *Ś.Br.*, 1:8:11.

64 *Ibid.*, *VII*, 5:1:5.

65 *MHB.* XII. 339, 103—4.

66 *Agni Purāṇa*, IV. 7.

67 *Manu*, 1, 5, 19; *Taitt. Brāhmaṇa*, 1·1·3·5.

To be more exact they were in the transition stage from water to land animals. With the ushering in of the Mesozoic, the reptiles 'began to stand up and go stoutly on all fours'. Of this class many divisions are distinguished including that of tortoise and turtles. Again hundreds of thousands of years roll on, and the end of the Mesozoic period witnesses theriomorphous reptiles, the ancestors of mammals. This leads us to the third and by far the most important division of the life-cycle portrayed by the geological record, the Cainozoic period. Here "a gigantic crumpling of the earth's crust and an upheaval of the mountain ranges was in progress. The Alps, the Andes, the Himalayas[68] are all Cainozoic mountain ranges."[69] Now appear thick forests and vast plains with vegetation (udbhijja) quite fit for the breed of a variety of mammals, (Jarāyuja)[70] Among the other oligocene mammals appears the giant pig.[71] To conclude the story of a life cycle, the age of the mammals is replaced by the Glacial Age where we have to mark the origin of man or at least manlike creatures. We cannot say how many thousands of years were covered by the Glacial Age where we meet with cave men, fishermen and sub-men. The first true men are seen in the Palaeolithic age. "It

68 For the three phases of upheaval of the Himalayas, See Wadia, *Geology of India*, pp. 202 ff. See also Oldham. *A Manual of the Geology of India*, Ch. XVIII. The age and origin of the Himalayas.

69 H. G. Wells, *op. cit.*, pp. 53—54.

70 As their name implies the mammals are the mothers par excellence.. Association and mutual aid are the rule with them. See H. F. Standing—*Spirit in Evolution*, (London, 1930), pp. 143 and 167.

71 H. G. Wells, *op. cit.* plate on p. 54.

was during these ages (the Tertiary era) that the most important surface features of the area were acquired, and the present configuration of the country (India) was outlined."[72] This synchronises with the Human Epoch which is distinguished by the presence of Man.

The cult of the fish.

The above outline of the life history from the point of view of a geologist is not out of place here as we shall see below. In its historical setting the conception of Daśāvatāra seems to be based on the evolution of the human race to which our ancient sages and seers appear to have been alive. The first among the incarnations is said to be the fish. The legend of the fish, as told in the Matsya Purāṇa, has already been noticed. That there was a fish cult in the ancient world[73] is seen from the sacred fish in the temples of Apollo and Aphrodite at Myra and Hieropolis, and from the fact that Dagon with a human head and hands was regarded as fish god. It is said that "Fish are kept in parts of Wales to give oracles."[74] It became later on the emblem of the

72 D. N. Wadia, *Geology of India*, (Macmillan, 1919), p. 203.

Prof. R. Gopala Iyer of the Department of Zoology of the University of Madras in an informing note says: "Man came on the scene very late. This was certainly after the formation of the big mountains. It is a moot question whether he was present when the great Himalayas were formed." I owe to Prof. Gopala Iyer for valuable suggestions in this section.

73 Profoundly interesting it is to know that drawings of fish, among others, believed to have been drawn by the Aurignacian artist of the Upper Palaeolithic epoch, are seen in the cave of Niaux, situated in one of the valleys of the Pyranees. (See W. J. Sollas, *Ancient Hunters*, p. 235 f. (Macmillan, 1911).

74 See *Enc. Religion and Ethics*, pp. 514—5.

Pāṇḍya monarchs of Tamil India, as testified by literary tradition and as is seen abundantly engraved on the architectural monuments like the temples left to us by ancient kings as permanent traces of their existence.[75]

What is still more interesting is that an image of fish is worshipped as Viṣṇu even today in the temple of Tiruvallam, better known as the Paraśurāma Temple, five miles to the south of Trivandrum and very near the sea, suggesting that it was once a shore temple. The antiquity of this temple cannot in any way be disputed. Apart from the Paraśurāma shrine, there are three separate shrines for Brahmā, Śiva and Viṣṇu in the same compound suggesting the once prevalent Trinity form of worship. The worship of the Triad is long before the waves of sectarianism swept over this part of the globe and we are not aware of any similar temple in other parts of South India where the worship of the Trinity is made in one and the same temple. The temple at Tiruvallam has a peculiar style of architecture which we may call the Malabar style. But to our purpose it is worthy of note that the image of Viṣṇu in this temple is that of Fish which raises a presumption of a cult of man-fish.

The Kūrma and Vārāha Avatārs.

The next incarnations in the traditional order are the Kūrma (tortoise) and Vārāha (the boar). In the progress of the life cycle these two incarnations suggest

75 See also Q.J.M.S. XIII, pp. 549—54, *Fish and Religion in South India.*

the amphibian and mammal stage of the record of the rocks. In the former we see the tortoise and in the latter we notice the giant pig. Though the legends behind these two incarnations are not furnished by the Purāṇa under reference, still there are other Purāṇas where the legend is given in full detail.[76] While the Kūrma legend reflects the stage of evolution of the aṇḍaja and udbhijja creatures and plants of the Mesozoic era,[77] the theriomorphic Vārāha[78] belongs to the category of what the Natural Historians of Sanskrit literature call the Jarāyuja. The idea behind the Boar incarnation is that the earth has crumbled owing to nature's havoc, like earthquakes and volcanoes, and the consequent upheaval of the earth's crust. This state of affairs, geologists tell us, covered hundreds of thousands of years of the Cainozoic, otherwise called the Tertiary epoch. The legend in the Purāṇa is that while the Earth was plunged into the nether world (pātāla) by the asura, the Lord in the shape of Boar got there and raised the earth's crust with the help of his Tusks to its original level.[79]

Narasimha and Vāmana Avatārs.

The next two incarnations in the accepted order are Narasimha (half-man and half-lion) and Vāmana (the dwarf). Charles Darwin taught that man is a

76 See for instance, the Kūrma Purāṇa and the Vārāha Purāṇa.

77 See Muir, O.S.T. Vol. I.; Agni P. 1:14; Viṣṇu P. 1:4.

78 Muir, *Ibid*, p. 63.

79 Ch. 247, 8.

descendant of a man-like ape.[80] If the 'dwarf' manifestation can be identified with the subman, the half-man the half-lion stage is to be the precursor of man-kind as against the Ape theory of modern scientists.[81] And this can be traced to the period of Cave men and Bushmen.

The Missing Link.

Thus the ancient Indian conceptions of the Daśāvatār has supplied the 'missing link'. The dwarf-man or the subman as the anthropologists will style him, can bear resemblance to Vāmana, the legend of whose incarnation is described in the Purāṇa.[82] Prahlāda says that He is the source of this entire universe. What is more interesting is the idea of a birth by the union of the mythical man and woman, Kaśyapa and Aditī. The incarnations previous to this are *ayonija,* in the sense that their origin was not due to the result of man joining his wife in wedlock. Kaśyapa is the mythical progenitor of all kinds of creatures in the world, and Vāmana, his son[83] represents the type of first man, a stage when the true man is yet a fact of the distant future.

Paraśurāma and Rāmacandra Avatārs.

We have next the manifestations of Paraśurāma and Rāmacandra. The symbol of Paraśu or axe with

80 See his *Descent of Man.*

81 *Nṛsimha Pūrva Tāpini Upaniṣad,* II, 5.

82 See Ch. 244 ff.

83 *Ibid.*

Rāma, the son of Jamadagni, shows the beginnings of a simple civilisation when man was still leading a nomad life and was primarily a hunter to begin with. From the man of the woods the true man comes into existence, and anticipates the civilised man of the city with all its amenities. The hero of the epic Rāmāyaṇa is the type of stalwart man, belonging to what is known as the Aryan race. This incarnation is followed by that of Kṛṣṇa and the Buddha. Kalki is yet a thing of very distant future.

Conclusion.

Every avatār then represents a distinct stage in the story of evolution of life. The most powerful of creatures of the respective epochs was looked upon with awe and veneration. A large number of legends grew around it or him as years rolled on, and a cult came to be definitely established. With the founding of a cult, tradition comes into the world and becomes the foundation of all religions in the world. Thus to the creatures of the palaeozoic period the man-fish was the god. This tradition came to stay as a permanent factor. In that way in every transitional stage, a new cult centres round the more powerful among the living creatures then. This resulted in a traditional lore, more varied and more numerous. This floating tradition gathered in volume in the course of aeons and came to be transmitted orally from generation to generation. Barring that which became lost and forgotten, the remnant of the lore came to be written in the later Purāṇic and Itihāsa books. Some also find mention in the Vedic works, especially those which go by the name of the Brāhmaṇas. Thus there is some justification for the statement contained in this Purāṇa and in the Vāyu Purāṇa that the Purāṇa is older than the Veda and that both are revealed texts.[84] Tradition may have originated in history or in romance. In this particular case, apart from the rational explanation of the Hindu theory of incarnation, idea is deep rooted among the Hindus that these ten incarnations are the different manifestations of the Lord Viṣṇu, one among the three principal Gods who go to make up the Hindu Trinity.

84 Vā. P. I. 60: See also my paper on the *Purāṇas a study*—in the *Ind. His. Quarterly*, (1932), p. 752.

CHAPTER II.

THE DATE OF THE PURĀṆA.

As in the case of the Vāyu Purāṇa the scene of the Purāṇa is laid in the sacred forest of the Naimiṣa where many of the great sages of India assembled to witness the sacrifice of Adhisīmakṛṣṇa, the Paurava king of much celebrity. Hence what follows in the dynastic accounts of reigning kings is recounted as it were in a prophetic tone, the kings of the 'future'. This list of 'future' kings is continued till the last of the kings of the Andhra dynasty. The Guptas are not mentioned, and this gives the certain clue to the fact that the last redaction of the Matsya Purāṇa must have taken place not later than the commencement of the Gupta epoch and immediately after the dismemberment of the Andhra empire. The latest date for the Purāṇa must be found somewhere towards the close of the third century as the Guptas commenced their rule from about 320 A.D.

Difficulty in fixing the earliest date

But this does not solve the problem. The real difficulty lies in fixing its upper limit. In its own words the Purāṇa contains 14,000 stanzas,[1] and has been compiled or to be more correct, has been narrated by

1 Ch. 53, 51. According to the Ānandāśrama edition, the actual stanzas are 14026.

Lomaharṣaṇa, a contemporary of Adhisīmakṛṣṇa, and a devoted pupil of sage Vyāsa.[2] The Purāṇa definitely says that Adhisīmakṛṣṇa was the reigning king by the use of the significant expression *sāṁpratam,* and Adhisīmakṛṣṇa was no doubt a historical person.[3] Pargiter would assign 850 B.C. as the approximate mean date of the beginning of his reign. But some writers are more liberal and push him back by a few more generations. If we are to credit the internal evidence of this Purāṇa, the bulk of the Purāṇa must have been composed then. Subsequently additions were made from time to time until the beginnings of the Gupta era, when possibly the extant version of the Purāṇa was reduced to writing.

Posterior to the Śatapatha Brāhmaṇa.

The additions are clearly in evidence as we shall presently notice. At the outset it must be conceded that the Purāṇa is quite familiar with the Vedic literature as such. It quotes now and then Vedic texts from the different *saṁhitās* and many important Upaniṣads. Especially is this so in dealing with a number of *vratams* or votive offerings with which the Purāṇa is full. It is unmistakable, as we have already seen, that the legendary account of the floods as contemplated by this Purāṇa is not original, and one has to look elsewhere for its origin. It is certainly supplied by the simple and

2 Ch. 50. 68.

3 See, for example, E. J. Rapson in the *Cam. H. of India,* Vol. I, p. 302, F. E. Pargiter: *An His. Tradition,* p. 182. Pradhan: *Chronology of An. India,* p. 254 ff.

matter-of-fact account furnished by the Śatapatha Brāhmaṇa, forming part of the Yajurveda. It can, therefore, be safely assumed that the Matsya Purāṇa was posterior to the composition of the Śatapatha Brāhmaṇa.

Anterior to Gṛhya Sūtras.

Apart from Vedic literature the Purāṇa shows immediate acquaintance with the Dharma and Gṛhya Sūtras of Āśvalāyana to a greater extent, and of Āpastamba to a smaller extent. The Purāṇa, which has a disorderly and confused section on the *pravaras* and *gotras* of the sages, seems to presuppose those well-marked lists in the epoch-making works of Baudhāyana and Āpastamba.[4] In point of injunctions, especially with regard to the ceremonies in honour of the deceased ancestors, the Purāṇa largely follows the early Dharma-sūtras and initiates certain injunctions which are either not contemplated by the law-codes or have become defunct in course of time. In Chapter (18) it refers to the practice, incumbent on householders of annual *ekoddiṣṭam* to the departed manes. In practice this is done on the 12th day after the decease of a certain person once and for all. Again in its recommendation of what is known as *āmaśrāddham,* which has now completely gone out of use, the Purāṇa puts on an air of

4 Chapters 195—203 require a careful reconstruction of the texts and proper editing. It is not possible, as it is, to spot out the gotra from pravara. A number of names of sages are jumbled together. No clear distinction is made out of ekārṣeya, trayārṣeya, pañcārṣeya, where three sages and five sages are to be mentioned. More than the number are given. Sometimes the number is indefinite. For a correct list see Āpa. Śrauta sūtra, 24, 5 f. Cp. *Skanda* P., III. Dharmāraṇya Kāṇḍa.

antiquity about it. Another recommendation that is almost extinct today is the offering of *piṇḍanirvāpanam* in the Agni or sacred fire.[5] But this has been at present restricted to the Kṣētra piṇḍam or the offering of rice balls in places of pilgrimage, or sacred tīrthas. In these particulars the Purāṇa can lay a claim of priority to the accepted codes like the Dharmaśāstras of Yājñavalkya and Manu.

Post-Pāṇinian.

The Purāṇa further mentions the names of Vyāghrapāda, Patañjali, and Kātyāyana the prominent grammarians of early Sanskrit. We know at least approximately the date of Patañjali to be 150 B.C. But authors earlier than Patañjali are also referred to in the Purāṇa, for example, Yāska, the author of an Arthaśāstra, Bābhravya and Bharata of the Nāṭyaśāstra fame. The reference to Yāska[6] is perhaps to the celebrated author of the *Nirukta*, who flourished somewhere about 500 B.C. He was the representative of a grammatical school which was willing to include in its work, usages of different Vedas and different schools of the same Veda.[7] One peculiar feature of this Purāṇa is the less number of archaic expressions and Vedic usages of which the Vāyu Purāṇa is full. This postively demonstrates that the science of grammar of the School of Pāṇini had been long in

5 Ch. 18, 27.

6 Ch. 195—36.

7 Keith, *A History of Sanskrit Literature*, p. 403.

existence before portions of the Purāṇa were reduced to the present form.

References to Arthaśāstra and Bābhravya Pāñcāla.

Between the author of the *Nirukta* and the author of the *Mahābhāṣya*, the quickening impulse of intellectual life has led to a host of invaluable works, which may very well come under the category of the scientific literature. But it must be noted, however, that though there was a tendency for the separation of religious from secular law in this new process of development, it was never realised. As Prof. Keith has pertinently remarked "there is no doubt of the dominant influence of religion on the growth of Sanskrit literature".[8] The outstanding output of this period consisted of the Arthaśāstra of Kauṭalya, the Kāmasūtra of Vātsyāyana and the Bharatīya Nāṭyaśāstra. The Arthaśāstra is mentioned in more than one place in the Matsya Purāṇa.[9] It is said that the mythical Budha learnt this science as well as other sciences which included the science of elephants (*hasti śāstram*) and of horses. Among the curricula of studies for a royal Prince the prescription laid down in the Kauṭalīya Arthaśāstra finds a prominent mention. The discussion centring round the *trivarga* which constitutes dharma, artha, and kāma in the chapters especially of 144 and 220, is in close imitation of that found in the Kauṭalīya. Also the prescriptions even of an ethical nature, that the mother though fallen from her virtues (*patita*) must still be

8 *Ibid.*, p. 406.

9 VII, 63, X, 32, XXIV, 2; cxliv, 22; ccxx, 2.

protected by the son,[10] that Dharma ought never to be neglected,[11] and that punishment should be meted out according to the gravity of offences bear infallible testimony that the author of the Purāṇa has chiefly followed Kauṭalya and his celebrated śāstra. In fact it was the first scientific work in the field of politics in classical times. The Arthaśāstra has been assigned on conclusive evidence to the reign of Candragupta Maurya c. 324 B.C.[12] Vātsyāyana is mentioned by name. But whether the author of the Kāmasūtra is under reference in these places[13] is a matter of opinion. As the name is celebrated as a *gotrapravartaka,* and as is often alleged on the testimony of the later Kośa literature like Abhidhānacintāmaṇi, that Kauṭalya and Vātsyāyana may be one and the same person, one may treat this reference, though with great caution, as pointing to the author of the Kāmasūtra.

But what is still more important to a student of history is the reference to Bābhravya as the author of a treatise on the Kāmasūtra which is unfortunately lost to us.[14] From the stanza[15] following this reference, one has to infer that he

10 Ch. 227, 150.

11 Ch. 201, 6.

12 See my *Mauryan Polity*, 1932, ch. I.

13 Ch. 196, 33 and ch. 199, 6.

14 Ch. 21, 30.

कामशास्त्रप्रणेताच बाभ्रव्यस्तु सुबालकः
पाञ्चाल इतिलोकेषु विश्रुतः सर्वशास्त्रवित् ॥

15 कण्डरीकोऽपिधर्मात्मा वेदशास्त्रप्रवर्तकः
भूत्वा जातिस्मरौ शोकात्पतितावग्रतस्तदा ॥

was a contemporary of a certain Kaṇḍarīka, or Kaṇḍīraka, a Vedic sage and perhaps an author of a Dharmaśāstra. But what we are concerned with at present is that this Bābhravya is accepted as an ancient authority on the Arthaśāstra and the Kāmaśāstra by both Kauṭalya and Vātsyāyana. Towards the end of the Kāmasūtra, Vātsyāyana acknowledges his indebtedness to him very handsomely.

बाभ्रवीयांश्च सूत्रार्थान् आगमय्यविमृश्यच

वात्स्यायनश्चकारेदं कामसूत्रं यथाविधि ॥

Besides this bald statement, the Kāmasūtra refers to Bābhravya's work in more than ten places. There were a number of disciples of Bābhravya. These, like Dattaka, Cārāyaṇa and others took up different aspects of his treatise in sūtra form and enlarged them without sacrificing the spirit of the original. Vātsyāyana, for example, from his own version follows completely and closely Bābhravya in his section entitled the *sāmprayōgika* which covers well nigh one-fourth of the book. It is significant that the Matsya Purāṇa calls him Bābhravya Pāñcāla,[16] with an attribute *sarvaśāstravit.*

The term Pāñcāla is interesting in our enquiry. In the Ṛgprātiśākhya, a certain Bābhravya figures as the author of the Kramapāṭha of the Ṛgveda and the commentator speaks of him as Bābhravya Pāñcāla. This has led Prof. Weber to postulate a theory that the Pāñcāla kingdom was the original home where the text of the Ṛgveda was rearranged and fixed in proper order.[17] It

16 Ch. 21. St. 30.

17 *History of Ind. Literature*, pp. 10 and 34; See also *Mhb. Śānti.*, Ch. 352, 37—38 (Kumbakonam Ed.).

is believed that the appellation of catuṣṣaṣṭi, or 64 varieties of *Sāmprayoga* or marital intercourse bear resemblance to eight aṣṭakas of eight chapters which give 64, and which constitute the *ṛks* of the ten *maṇḍalas.* But this is clearly a far-fetched statement. It may be that Bābhravya is the author of the Kramapāṭha and of a science on erotics as well. As this theory hangs on the slender creeper of the appellation catuṣṣaṣṭi, it is susceptible to break down at any stage.

It has been again surmised that the Pāñcāla country was perhaps the part of the Indian continent where the science of erotics was specially cultivated.[18] This is not the time or place to discuss such details of a controversial nature. But what is relevant to our purpose is that Bābhravya is an old teacher, and perhaps a Ṛṣi, who lived long before the composition of Vātsyāyana's classical work, the Kāmasūtra. It is worthy of note that the Purāṇa does not make particular mention of this latter work.

Reference to Nāṭya Śāstra.

Among other scientific works which the Purāṇa mentions is the Nāṭyaśāstra of Bharata. The Purāṇa styles it as the Bharata Śāstra. Incidentally we are told that Bharata is the author of a dramatic work called Lakṣmīsvayamvaram. This is introduced as having been actually enacted in the immediate presence of the author Bharata, Menakā, Urvaśī, and Rambhā

18 See H. C. Chakladar—*Studies in Vāts. Kāmasūtra* (Greater India Soc. Public. No. 3), 1929, *Cal.* pp. 5 ff.

taking part in it. But Urvaśī whose heart was after the king Purūravas and who acted the part of Lakṣmī did not do it in the manner prescribed by Bharata. This enraged Bharata who cursed her to become a creeper and Purūravas to be an aerial spirit, and that was to continue to a period of 55 years. The story goes that when the period of the curse was over, Urvaśī became the mother of eight children through Purūravas.[19] This legend reminds us of a similar account in the Tamil classical literature. When once Urvaśi misbehaved in the heavenly sabhā, by setting her love towards Indra's son Jayanta, she and Jayanta were similarly cursed. She became a dancing girl of the earth and he was born as a bamboo stick on the Vindhyas.[20]

This digression apart, we have the unimpeachable authority of the Purāṇa itself to show that the Purāṇa was posterior at least in certain portions to the scientific works of Bharata, the great master of music and dancing. Of these the extant work is his Nāṭyaśāstra.[21] It is worthy of note that in narrating the legend of Urvaśī the Purāṇa calls special attention to the *abhinaya* of Bharata. And we know that the Nāṭyaśāstra is of four books treating on the four *abhinayas*—śātvika, aṅgika, vācika and āhārya. These are translated as 'a mode conveyed by the effort of the mind, by the natural movements of the organs, by the delivery through expression and by the dress, deport-

19 Ch. 24, 28 ff.

20 See my *Studies in Tamil Literature and History*, pp. 288-89.

21 In the course of publication in the Gaekwad Oriental Series, Baroda, edited by M. Rāmakrishna Kavi, with the commentary of Abhinava Gupta.

ment and mise-en-scene'.[22] Thus we are led to infer that the work under reference in the Purāṇa is that in which the doctrine of Rasa or sentiment which is developed in the extant Nāṭyaśāstra with its eight sub-divisions is well known to the compiler of the Purāṇa. When Umā (the dark-hued) got herself transformed into Gaurī (the white) and entered the residence of Rudra, the latter assumed the form of Bhairava with the doctrine of sentiment predominating (*rasa*). The eight elements that constitute this sentiment are erotic, comic, pathetic and those of horror, heroism, fear, disgust, and wonder.

सकामःशङ्कितोदीनो रौद्रोवीरो भयानकः
करुणाहास्यबीभत्स किंचित्किंचिद्रसोऽभवत् ॥

This sentiment is a feeling, which according to later authorities, 'is purely an emotion comparable to the bliss obtained in contemplation of the absolute by the intellect which can comprehend it.'.[23] This treatise of dramaturgy can be roughly assigned to a period earlier than the dramatist Bhāsa and the still greater Kālidāsa whose dates are still subjects of controversy among scholars.[24] Bharata, whom later tradition furnishes the status of Muni or sage, is undoubtedly an ancient author, much reputed in his time.

22 *Ibid*, Vol. I, Intro. p. 7.

23 Keith, *A History of Sans. Lit.*, p. 373. Cf. also his *Sanskrit Drama*, 1924, pp. 314 ff.

24 The late Gaṇapati Śāstri places Bhāsa in the 5th Century B.C. though others are inclined to fix him in the early centuries of the Christian era. Mr. K. S. Rāmaswāmi Śāstri assigns Kālidāsa to the 2nd B.C. (see his *Kālidāsa*, Ch. V, (1933).

References to other scientific works.

The Purāṇa goes to mention, again, other scientific works in medicine, astrology, and astronomy, architecture and sculpture. Indian tradition traces the Āyurveda as an upāṅga of the Atharvaveda. The sage Dhanvantari is designated as the progenitor of this branch of Indian science.[24a] Him the Purāṇa styles Bhagavān in view of the fact that he is looked upon as an avatār of Viṣṇu, and that the purpose of the incarnation is said to have been to fight out diseases and endow man and beast with sound health. The Purāṇa indulges in a mythical origin of the first author of Indian medicine. It is said that among the persons and things which came out of the churning of the ocean, Dhanvantari was one. Bereft of its mythical character the fact seems to be that Dhanvantari was the first teacher of the science of Āyurveda. Possibly he was a historical personage who flourished in the epoch of the Atharva Veda. We have today an old medical glossary attributed to this reputed author. The lexicon goes by the name of *Dhanvantari Nighaṇṭu*,[25] and seems to be much more ancient than the *Amarakōśa,* though the spurious legend of Vikramāditya of Ujjayinī makes them contemporaries.[26]

Astronomical data.

Though the Purāṇa refers to the mean motions of the sun and the moon as well as the five-year yuga and other details which cover the field of astronomy, and though it commends auspicious time for the making of

24a Ch. 251. 1.

25 Ed. *An. Sans. Series*, 33, 1896.

26 See Weber, Z.D.M.G., 22, 708—18, Fleet, *Ind. Ant.*, Vol. 30, 3 f.

gifts, for the performance of rituals, for the march of the king which cover the relative field of astrology, and though the calculation of yugas, manvantaras, kalpas, and the age of seven ṛṣis and of Brahmā is furnished in detail, we refrain from examining these here for the simple reason that such portions as deal with them are not legitimately of this Purāṇa but are of the Vāyu Purāṇa.[27]

Being a mere copy of an older text these portions are of no value in fixing the provisional chronological scheme of the Matsya Purāṇa. It is, however, of interest to note that the Purāṇa in its reference to holy baths at the different sacred spots in and around the Narmadā region makes mention of the *Aṅgāraka dina*[27a] besides the tithi, pakṣa, māsa and ayana of the year. The mention of this week-day is important as it is generally believed that it was a later growth in the tree of Indian astronomical science.[28] In this connection mention may be made of the significance the Purāṇa attaches to dreams and their effects, suggesting an age of crude astrology, and consequently of superstitious ideas and beliefs reminding us of the *kānānūl* in vogue in the ancient Tamil land.

Evidence of Architecture.

The other field of scientific learning in which the Purāṇa indulges is architecture and town planning. It is called Vāstuvidyā and usually Śilpaśāstra. It

27 An outline of these details is given in a section in my *Some Aspects of the Vāyu Purāṇa*, Madras University, 1933.

27a Ch. 193-8.

28 See Q.J.M.S., Oct., 1920, p. 72.

is the science of the architect. The Mānasāra seems to be an authority among the earlier works of this class. But it is very difficult to fix a definite date of its compilation.[29] There is again the Maya Śāstra, and if the evidence of the Tamil Śangam classics can be cited, this must have been in vogue much earlier than the commencement of the Christian era. The legendary activities of this Maya, the architect of the Asuras as opposed to Viśvakarmā, the architect of the Devas, can be gathered from the description of the Tripuram and other buildings connected with it in the Matsya Purāṇa. To a student of history Maya is an author on the science of architecture who differs in certain principles from the traditional regulations laid down, similarities apart. Though these treatises are of uncertain date, the data furnished by the Purāṇa in regard to palace buildings, temple building, and image making, presuppose a full-fledged culture like that of Mohenjodaro and Harappa in the chalcolithic period, which has compelled students of Indian chronology to revise their dating with regard to many things. By referring to this we do not propose to find any connecting link between the prescriptions of the Purāṇa and the early Indus culture, though it is not impossible.

There is evidence, in this Purāṇa of the *Śikhara* style of architecture, which, according to Codrington, is a much later style. This mere theorising of the Purāṇa has been corroborated by the known Gupta *Śikhara*

29 See P. K. Acharya—*Architecture of Mānasāra*, Preface, pp. lvi, ff. (Oxford).

temples as illustrated by the Deo-Barnarak temples and the Mahadeopur temple in the district of Shahabad in Bihar. Mr. K. P. Jayaswal draws our attention again to the *śikhara* in the Bodhgaya plaque which is in terracotta bearing an inscription of the second century A.D..[30] These are not all. Among the minor sciences of which the Matsya Purāṇa is full, one can mention in a categorical order the science of archery (Dhanurveda), the science connected with the training and healing of horses,[31] and of elephants[32] and of painting and of music. It includes magic arts like Sañjīvini vidyā and Vākovākya. While the first three are known to the author of the Kauṭalīya, the next two, are known to the author of the Kāmasūtra. This means that such sciences were in a developed stage in the fourth century B.C. and before. The last two of the list deserve some notice.

The Sañjīvini Vidyā belongs purely to the realm of magic. It is a science, a knowledge of which equips one with the power to give life to the dead person. It is said in the Purāṇa that Śukrācārya, the purohita of the Asuras, learnt this mysterious science from no less a person than Śiva after severe austerities, and was able to revive to life the hosts of the Asuras who fell a prey to the sword of the Devas in the so-called Devāsura battles.[33] Again it appears that there were people in ancient India who could study and understand the language of

30 See the *Modern Review*, Aug. 1932, p. 150.

31 Ch. 215, 38.

32 Ibid, 36.

33 Ch. 25, 65: cp. *Brahmāṇḍa*, P. Ch. 40, 52.

the birds and beasts. It is said that Brahmadatta, the Pāñcāla king, had a knowledge of this śāstra (*satva ruta*). Once while witnessing in the presence of his wife, a love quarrel between two ants, he burst into a laugh. The latter, who was not aware of this fact, took this seriously. For she thought that her husband was laughing at her and without being convinced of his words as to the reason why he laughed, she left him in disgust.[34] This story goes to illustrate that such knowledge of the languages of the birds and animals was the privilege only of a few, and was not shared by all. Unfortunately this art had become almost extinct in India. It is not clear whether the expression Vākovākya of the Upaniṣads is after all a reference to this science of the language of the dumb creatures.[35] In a note[36] Dr. Keith remarks 'vakovākya perhaps denotes the dialogues which develop into philosophy'. It was pointed out in my *Hindu Administrative Institutions*[37] that the expression means the language of animals. As there were specialists who knew such languages, Kauṭalya recommends that the council chamber was to be inaccessible not only to man but also to birds and beasts.[38] What we wish to emphasise is that the term has a special value of its own, and means something very different from what Prof. Keith suggests. The assumption is that this art was prevalent in the epic and the Kauṭalīyan epoch, and came to be forgotten

34 Ch. 20 and 21.

35 See *Chāndogya* Up. III, 11, 2; cp. *Mahābhāṣya*, I, 9.

36 *A History of Sanskrit Literature*, p. 8.

37 pp. 136 & 137.

38 Bk. I Sec. 15.

afterwards as there is no warrant in later literature of its being used. The same holds good with regard to experts in the language of plants.

The Purāṇa and the Epics.

The Purāṇa shows in different places of its acquaintance with the epic literature. Both the itihāsas, the Rāmāyaṇa and the Mahābhārata are known to the Purāṇa by name. In some places the Purāṇa quotes the very passage from these epics that one has to conjecture that the extant works of the Rāmāyaṇa of Vālmīki and the Mahābhārata were known to the author of the Matsyapurāṇa. Though no final word has been said with regard to the chronology of these epics, it is generally admitted on all hands that the major portion of the itihāsas must be assigned to a much older date. It would be safe to conclude that 'the latest sūtras and the epics belong to the same period' inasmuch as one finds a close connection between the two styles of literature, besides the common list of teachers and teachings in them.[39] In the Matsya Purāṇa we have the following statements:

Bhāratākhyānamakhilam cakre tadupabṛmhitam|
Lakṣeṇaikena yatproktam vedārtha paribṛmhitam||
Ch. 53—70

This bears testimony to the fact that the Bhārata has been classified as an ākhyāna or historical story, and its didactic portions follow the Vedic injunctions, and that it is a composition containing one lakh of verses. The

39 C.H.I, Vol. 1, p. 252.

mention of this figure is significant. The extant recension, called Southern recension is believed to contain interpolations of a varied character, added on to the original text from time to time and hence contains a hundred thousand verses.[40] The Matsya Purāṇa itself admits of a Bhārata with a lakh of verses in length. This means that the extant Bhārata, of the Southern recension was known to the compiler of the Matsya Purāṇa. As the lowest limit of the Purāṇa cannot be later than 300 A.D. the epic in its present form existed in the early centuries of the Christian era at the least, and it was not tampered with afterwards.[41] The next statement of the Purāṇa is still more interesting:—

Vālmīkinā tu yatproktam rāmopākhyānamuttamam|
Brahmaṇābhihitam yacca śatakoṭipravistaram||
Āhṛtya nāradāyaiva tena vālmīkaye punaḥ|
Vālmīkināca lokeṣu dharmakāmārthasādhanam||
Evam sapādāh pañcaite lakṣāh martye prakīrtitāh||
Ch. 53, St. 71—72.

Brahmā, the creator, composed the story of Rāma elaborately in a hundred crores of verses. Nārada learnt this and spoke to Vālmīki about it. Vālmīki in his turn condensed it into five lakhs, and one-fourth for the benefit of the humanity in its realisation of the trivarga—dharma, artha and kāma. While one notices the ascending order of accumulation of centuries in the Great Epic, here we have the descending order followed through ages. Here

40 See Hopkins, C.H.I. 1, pp. 255—6.

41 Ch. 53, p. 70.

was no addition to the original epic text, but a condensation or an epitomisation of the longer version into a short one. If orthodox tradition is to be believed, two hands were at work in this process of condensation. If we try to lift the veil of the dubious origin of this epoch-making kāvya called usually the *Ādikāvya* we can credit Vālmīki as a historical person, and a contemporary of Rāma, the hero of the epic, Rāmāyaṇa. A sage who lived in the forest, not far from Ayodhyā, and who was responsible for the upbringing of the two boys, Kuśa and Lava, the sons of Rāma, until they grew to manhood, must have had an intimate knowledge of the life of Rāma, and could, therefore, speak with first hand knowledge. To a student of ancient India the Rāmāyaṇa furnishes genuine and authoritative material. This apart, the age of Vālmīki is our main problem. According to Pargiter, Rāma lived in the fifth century before the great war of the Mahābhārata which he fixes provisionally 1100 B. C.[42] If this dating be accepted, Vālmīki who was Rāma's contemporary must have flourished about 1600 B.C., and the Rāmāyaṇa which he compiled was handed down by tradition until it was reduced to writing in the sūtra period. Logically there is a plausibility about this theory. From the foregoing discussion one thing is certain and it is that our Purāṇa must be a little later than the latest sūtra period, to which the epics are assigned on acceptable grounds.

Its relation to other Purāṇas.

The Matsya Purāṇa shows its indebtedness to other Purāṇas as well as the Dharmaśāstras. We have

42 *An Ind. His. Tradition*, Ch. XV.

already seen how this Purāṇa has completely followed the Vāyu version in chapters dealing especially with cosmogony, geography, astronomy, astrology and mathematics, as well as in giving an account of the dynasties of the Kali age as Pargiter would have it. It could not be the other way about viz., the Vāyu Purāṇa copying from the Matsya Purāṇa for reasons set forth in the previous section. Therefore we can logically conclude that the Matsya Purāṇa is later than the Vāyu version though the latter includes the Guptas in its account of the Kali dynasties.

The Matsya Purāṇa further shows its intimate acquaintance with the Bhāgavata Purāṇa. Scholars are not wanting to put forward a theory that the Bhāgavata Purāṇa is a much later work, perhaps of the 10th century A.D. and after, and it cannot find a legitimate place in the list of the so-called eighteen Mahāpurāṇas. The upholders of this theory are willing to include the Devi Bhāgavatam as one among the eighteen. This view is not convincing. This is not the place or time to examine the reasons for and against the theory. Suffice to say here that the tradition in the Bhāgavata Purāṇa does not warrant such a late date. All know that the writings of the philosopher Rāmānuja mark a definite stage in the religious beliefs of the Hindus. Up to his time it was a period of Bhakti or devotion to God or what one may call *abhedabuddhi* i.e. no sense of differentiation in the deities worshipped. After Rāmānuja though the kernel of the doctrine of the Bhakti was continued to be impressed, the *abhedabuddhi* gave place to *bheda-*

buddhi engendering in its train sectarianism and sectarian spirit in matters religious. The Bhāgavata Purāṇa is certainly a pre-Rāmānuja work. Like the Bhagavat Gītā it is terse and crisp. It is not sectarian in character though it deals elaborately with the ten incarnations of Viṣṇu. The deity Nārāyaṇa, who is glorified throughout, is none else than the one supreme God, who is usually called the Maheśvara. Like the Gītā it admits of interpretation from the *advaita, dvaita* and other points of view. It is as clear as day light that the Bhāgavata Purāṇa instructs *abheda-buddhi* in the matter of belief and worship. As such it claims a right place among the eighteen Mahāpurāṇas. If we now compare the texts of the Matsya Purāṇa with the Bhāgavata Purāṇa we find striking similarities in several particulars. The purpose of the Avatār of Matsya is not directly told in our Purāṇa. One has in vain to seek for it from its pages. Apart from the stray reference to the Hayagrīva episode[43] there is not the full and direct version. This is supplied by the Bhāgavata Purāṇa which enters into a disquisition as to the origin of the incarnation of the fish god. It was to recover the Vedas stolen by the demon Hayagrīva and taken away to the nether world.[44] It may be that the Bhāgavata Purāṇa supplemented what was actually wanting in the Matsya Purāṇa. Or, it may be that the compiler of the Matsya Purāṇa was aware of the detailed version in the Bhāgavata and did not want to repeat it once again.

43 Ch. 53. 5 and Ch. 261, 53—54.

44 See in this connection the I.H.Q., III, p. 4 ff.

The same doubt rises in another field of enquiry. In dealing with ways and means of warding off the evils as a consequence of bad dreams, the Purāṇa prescribes the hearing of the episode of Nāgendramōkṣa, the Gajendramokṣa of the Bhāgavata Purāṇa. In the Matsya Purāṇa or for the matter of that in its earlier contemporary, the Vāyu Purāṇa, we have no account of the Gajendramokṣa which is found in the Bhāgavata Purāṇa. When the Matsya Purāṇa enjoins definitely the hearing of that section dealing with the salvation of the elephant we have no other alternative than to conclude that the Purāṇa refers to the section in the Bhāgavata Purāṇa only. For we are not aware of any other ancient work where there is a fuller treatment of the tale regarded as fit for reading or hearing for sacerdotal purposes. This unmistakeable reference removes our difficulty once for all and indirectly helps us to fix an approximate date for the Bhāgavata Purāṇa also. It may, perhaps, be argued that this may be an interpolation. If it is so the Hayagrīva episode must also be an interpolation. Considering the religious and philosophical ideas much in common with the Matsya Purāṇa the conclusion forces itself that we need not suspect an interpolation.

References to Law-Codes.

The Purāṇa presupposes a number of law-codes as having been extant during the period of its composition by its frequent reference to the collective term Dharmaśāstra.[45] Mention is made of the law-givers like

45 See, for example, Ch. 182, 43.

Yājñavalkya and Manu. It is strange to note the silence of the Purāṇa with regard to the Parāśara smṛti, which, in the fitness of things, must be classed among the later law-codes. In its prescriptions on marriage and other aspects of social life the Purāṇa cites Manu as the primary authority.[46] But it is a moot question to answer whether such references are to the extant law-book attributed to Manu, or a bigger work and a much more ancient one attributed to a Bṛhat or Vṛddha Manu. One does not fail to notice that the same verses or a part of the verses are repeated in this Purāṇa from the extant text of Manu which, according to George Buhler, could be placed between 2nd Century B.C. and 2nd Century A.D.[47] The enunciation of the hypothesis that the original *Mānavadharma-sūtra* was reduced to metrical texts is not unconvincing. In this process of transformation it is but natural that sometimes the very sūtras are repeated in these metrical texts making it difficult for us to differentiate the older texts from the later and new additions. The reference to Yājñavalkya shows that Yājñavalkya cannot be a later writer as is sometimes held.

Jainism.

By far the most important is the fact that the Purāṇa furnishes an origin of Jainism. Once there was a war between the devas and the asuras. The chief part was played by Indra and Prahlāda respectively. At that time were flourishing the five sons of

46 Ch. 227, 27, and 113.

47 S.B.E. XXV, *Intro.*, pp. cxiv—cxv.

Nahuṣa, all Mahārathas. One among them was Rāji, a man who had attained much prowess by severe penance in honour of Nārāyaṇa. Knowing this Indra requisitioned his services. Rāji complied with his request. Vanquishing the asuras, he saw Indra once more in the possession of his kingdom. When Rāji retired to forest for a life of penance and prayer, his sons provoked Indra and deprived him of his status and kingdom. Indra appealed to his purohita Bṛhaspati. To get out of the deadlock the divine guru deluded the sons of Rāji by the teaching of Jīna dharma which was outside the pale of the orthodox Hinduism. This Jīna dharma constituted of *hetu vāda,* or the theory of ratiocination, as opposed to the faith in the Vedas as revealed texts. When Rāji's sons followed this cue and hence became fallen from the traditional path of righteousness, Indra conquered them and got back his original status of being the over-lord of the gods.[48]

Here is then a dubious origin of the Jaina faith. The value of this legendary account consists in the fact that the Jaina sect began in much earlier times, and that it discarded the authority of the Vedas. Though it began as an off-shoot of Brahmanism, the latter had to fight it out and establish itself once more safe and secure. Students of the history of ancient India know that Mahāvīra was the founder of this sect in the historical period, and that he flourished in the latter half of the sixth century B.C. The latest

48 Ch. 24, 34 ff.

researches assign 468 B.C. as the date of his death.[49] This prophet, according to Jaina tradition, is the 24th tīrthankara, the first being king Ṛṣabha, the father of Bharata, the first cakravartin of Ancient India. There has been an attempt to connect this Ṛṣabha with the kings of that name occurring in the Śatapatha Brāhmaṇa[50] or in the Aitareya Brāhmaṇa.[51] This is, indeed, far-fetched to begin with, and it may be that the Jains look upon Mahāvīra more as a reformer of their church than the original founder. If the reference in the Matsya Purāṇa is to the reformed sect of Mahāvīra, then, the Purāṇa is to be dated at least a few decades after 468 B.C.

Buddhism.

Of equal value is the reference to the Buddha, the younger contemporary of Mahāvīra.[52] The Purāṇa goes to the length of including the Buddha as one among the ten incarnations of Viṣṇu just after that of the Lord as Kṛṣṇa Vāsudeva. In this respect it totally agrees with the tradition transmitted by the Bhāgavata Purāṇa and the Agni Purāṇa. Evidently the Buddha's philosophical school had much in common with the later form of Vedic religion, that the later Hinduism recognised him among the Purāṇic pantheon. In fact the Buddha was a great philosopher and Yogin,

49 See *C.H.I.*, *Vol.* 1, p. 156.

50 XIII, 5—4—15.

51 VII, 17.

52 See for a full discussion of the dates of these prophets *Ind. Ant.*, 1914, Charpentier's article.

that made even Aśoka, the follower of the orthodox religion,[53] entitle him Bhagavān. This honorific title was earned by the great and exemplary sages of ancient India. For example, Dhanvantari was a Bhagavān. Vyāsa was one such. The school of Buddhism condemned by Śankara is a later growth, much deviated from the tenets and principles of the honoured founder.[54]

We again meet with the term Mahābodhi in the sense of a pitṛtīrtha fit for sacred bath and gift.[55] Perhaps it would be a far cry to look for its identification with Bodhi tree under which the Buddha is said to have attained his nibbana (*nirvāṇa*).[56] The term *nibbana* is interpreted also as arhantship. But there would be nothing strange in viewing this place as a sacred place of pilgrimage to all Hindus, for even today the practice is to visit this spot before the actual piṇḍa offerings are given on the banks of the Gayā. Thus the Matsya Purāṇa envisages a period when orthodox Hindu opinion was not different from the accepted Buddhist notions, and when the Buddha had attained the status of a Bhagavān at least by the time of Aśoka, the Mauryan emperor. For purposes of chronology this Purāṇa must be regarded as a work posterior to the age of the Buddha whose birth is provisionally fixed as 483 B.C. For various reasons into which we cannot

53 See my *Mauryan Polity*, sec. *Aśoka's Religion*.

54 See in this connection Mrs. Rhys Davids, *Gotama, the Man*, Luzac & Co. (London).

55 Ch. 22, 33.

56 *Digha* I, 115, II—151.

now enter the whole of the Purāṇa cannot be pre-buddhistic.

Other references—Upapurāṇas.

Many interesting data are found scattered in the pages of the Matsya Purāṇa which would go a long way in settling the uncertainty which centres round the chronology of the work. These are the worship of the moon as an independent deity, the reference to Vaikhānasa, the reference to Śukranīti, to Liṅgāyatana-ārādhyas, the worship of Vāsudeva, the Vāmaṇa temple, the betel leaf, the Upapurāṇas and the Ardhanārīśvara temples with Viṣṇu images. To take up, first, the Upapurāṇas. The Matsya Purāṇa mentions three of these by name. They are Nārasimham, Nandipurāṇa and Sāmbam. The position of the Upapurāṇas has been much misunderstood and this was particularly so because once the Purāṇas themselves were relegated to oblivion as untrustworthy material for purposes of history. Now that the ban has been lifted and the Purāṇa literature has been taken into account, the view with regard to the Upapurāṇas is likely to be changed. In any case the purpose of a researcher is to sift history from myth, to whatever class the literature may belong. The literature of the Upapurāṇas is as voluminous and as important to a student of tradition as the major Purāṇas themselves. It is to be viewed as different from the sthalamahātmyas or legendary origins of important centres of religious pilgrimages, which are very late in origin and which cannot be credited with much trustworthiness. Viewed in this light the Upapurāṇas must not be dismissed with passing mention. If the Matsya Purāṇa has any message to impart, it is that the Upapurāṇas are generally tacked on to a certain major Purāṇa, or form an important section of a major Purāṇa reducing themselves to the status of a minor Purāṇa or Upapurāṇa, when taken and studied alone. For example, the Nārasimha Purāṇa is claimed to be the section on Nārasimha's greatness in the major Padmapurāṇa. Thus the Upapurāṇas grew out of and sometimes with the major Purāṇas. Some of them seem to be anterior to certain of the major Purāṇas. If this view is taken, the chronological scheme becomes still more complicated, and the age of the Upapurāṇas has to be spread over a number of centuries. Unless we could treat the reference to three Upapurāṇas as strictly interpolations there is no escaping the fact that they precede the Matsya Purāṇa in point of chronology. From this, one thing is clear viz.: that portions of the Padma Purāṇa are more ancient than the Matsya Purāṇa.

Vaikhānasa Śāstra.

The reference to Vaikhānasa[57] is certainly interesting. The Purāṇa presupposes an elaborate form of image worship and equally elaborate details as to the architecture of temples. Intimately connected with

57 24:51.

यतिःकुमारभावेऽपि योगीवैखानसोऽभवेत् ॥

It is said that Yati, the eldest among the seven sons of Nahuṣa, became Vaikhānasa, and had no son to succeed him. Hence the next brother Yayāti became king.

temple worship is the rise of Āgama with its legacy of abundant literature. The āgama schools were Śaiva and Vaiṣṇava, and of these the Śiva āgamas were larger in number than the Vaiṣṇava āgama books. Among the latter, again, two schools are distinguished: the Pāñcarātra School[58] and the Vaikhānasa School. Luckily for us representative works of both these āgamas have been published, the *Ahirbudhnya* representing the former, and *Marici saṁhitā* the latter (published very recently by the Mahant of Tirupati). From the archaic nature of the expressions in the work and from the sūtra style, one has to infer very legitimately that the Vaikhānasa sūtras are much older than the Pāñcarātra texts. It is significant to note in this connection that Manu refers to the institutes of Vaikhānasa when he prescribes rules for the hermits of the forest.[59] Medhātithi comments:—

वैखानसं नाम शास्त्रं यत्रवानप्रस्थस्य धर्मान्विहितास्तेषां मते स्थितः ।

Other commentators on the Mānavadharma śāstra share this view of Medhātithi, and it is supposed that the institutes of Vikhānasa are more concerned with the regulations laid down for the people of the third āśrama, or the vānaprastha. This Vaikhānasa śāstra is undoubtedly, the sūtra promulgated by the sage Vaikhānas.[60] The antiquity of this work is attested

58 On this see F. O. Schrader, *Introduction to the Pāñcarātra and the Ahirbudhnya Samhita.*

59 VI, 21.

60 A Dharmasūtra is puplished under the title of *Vaikhānasa-dharmapraśna*, consisting of three praśnas dealing with castes, mixed castes and āśramas by T. Gaṇapati Sāstri in the *Trivandrum Sanskrit*

to by the unimpeachable reference to it in the Baudhāyanadharmasūtra.[61] George Buhler, in his introduction to the Laws of Manu, remarked that 'we may even hope to recover the work in course of time' a work that preceded the extant Manusmṛti.[62] As the work is now made available in print we hope further researches into that work will add to the sum total of our knowledge. Be this as it may, it seems certain that in the epoch of the Matsya Purāṇa and very much earlier, the Vaikhānasa school had come to stay, and the Pāñcarātra was yet a thing of the future.

Śukranīti?

Still more interesting is a reference, though indirect, to the political maxims of Śukrācārya. In the illuminating discussion that centres round the choice of the proper successor to the great Yayāti, it is contended by the representative bodies in the state that the eldest son was the legitimate successor. At that time Yayāti quotes the authority of what we can call the Śukranīti to the effect that[63] that son who is loyal to the reigning king, viz.: his father, must be anointed king. On this authority the Paura and Jānapada agree to crown the youngest Pūru, who alone of Yayāti's sons acted up to the wishes of his father. If this legend has anything of value, it is that according to the Purāṇa the Śukranīti

Series, No. 28, 1913. Attention may be drawn also to the *Vaikhānasa smārtasūtram*, translated by Dr. W. Caland and published by the Asiatic Society of Bengal, 1929. cp. also *Das Dharmasūtra der Vaikhānasas* by Wilhelm Eggers, Gottingen, 1929.

61 II, 11. 14, *S.B.E.*, Vol. XIV, p. 259.

62 *S.B.E.*, xxv, *Intro.*, pp. xxviii—xxix.

63 Ch. 34: 25.

is an ancient work. But we have to answer another question whether this is a reference to the extant Śukranīti. There is a school of opinion that this work must be a very late production, as late as the 12th century, as there is a reference to guns and gun powder. But one has to agree with K. P. Jayaswal in assigning considerable antiquity to the extant treatise of Śukra.[64] Whatever may be the correct interpretation of the term Śukra, in the Matsya Purāṇa in the passage under reference, one has to conjecture that the author of the Purāṇa knew of a Śukranīti though not identical with what we have. The latter is perhaps a relic of the old with considerable later additions by the redactors from time to time. The Purāṇa does a distinct service by claiming a great antiquity to Śukra's genuine work on the Nīti Śāstra.

The Lunar Cult.

There are other equally interesting data which may go a long way in settling the chronological limits of the Purāṇa. First is the worship of the moon as an independent deity. It has been contended that while the sun has attained the status of an independent deity, the moon does not seem to enjoy that status in the Hindu pantheon.[65]. It may be pointed out, to begin with, that the moon was worshipped as an independent diety in the Vedic and post-Vedic days including the age of the earlier Purāṇas. The *soma sūktam* and a number of fasts and votive offerings in honour of the moongod adumbrated in the Matsya Purāṇa, go to indicate that the Purāṇa recognises the moon as an independent deity

64 See my *Hindu Ad. Institutions*, p. 6, n. 4.

65 *Ind. Ant.*, Vol. 61, p. 17,

and in this respect follows the Vedic tradition.[66] It is true that in later days, not later than Varāhamihira, the celebrated authority on astronomy and astrology, the worship of the moon came to be merged as it were in that of the sun, and this practice began to gain ground from the 6th century A.D. But before this there was the moon cult and what is of absorbing interest is that the early Śangam literature of the Tamils corroborates the view that there were separate moon temples in the capitals of Tamil kingdoms dedicated to the worship of the moon. Though we have no temples extant solely dedicated to the moon, traces of ancient modes of worship of that deity still linger in the Tamil land. To cite an instance we have the *piṟaitoḻutal* or seeing the moon rise in the third day after the new moon day.[67]

It is curious and rather strange that the Matsya Purāṇa does not refer to the image of a moon in its long chapters on the making of images and building of temples. It may be that these portions are later additions if we are only to reconcile the earlier part where the worship of the moon is inculcated in detail. We have the prime authority of the Śangam literature that such separate worship was continued to the second and third centuries of the Christian era, if not later. In the light of the above remarks one has to infer that the Matsya Purāṇa belongs to the transitional period when the ancient Hindus were slowly discontinuing the wor-

66 cp. *Rāma.*, III, VI, 5.

67 See *Ind. Ant.*, Sep. 1933.

ship of the moon as an independent deity in separate temples built for the purpose.[68]

The Vāmana temple.

This is not the only example of a cult which was once prevalent and afterwards became defunct. The Purāṇa mentions a few more, and one such is the special temple dedicated to Vāmana. Once there seems to have been prevalent the practice of worshipping God in all His manifestations. We hear of the special temples for Narasimha, Vāmana, Vāsudeva, Trivikrama, Vārāha, Buddha, not to speak of other minor manifestations of Viṣṇu as Upendra, Balarāma, Pārthasārathi, and so on. In the march of time these temples had gone out of use, and the cults of Rāma and Kṛṣṇa became predominant and they came to be looked upon as harmless deities showering blessings to their devotees. But in the age when the Matsya Purāṇa was compiled, conditions were quite different. It was an age of religious fervour, and every individual had reason for his leanings towards the one or the other of the manifestations of the Lord. Hence a number of cults and numberless temples. The Matsya Purāṇa in one place glorifies Viṣṇu as Upendra,[69] and refers in the same chapter to the temple of Vāmana in the city of Kurukṣetra as flourishing in the days of the Pāṇḍavas of the Mahābhārata.[70] If the later literature and epigraphy can be the test, we do not hear of Vāmana temples in later days, though we hear of the Vārāha cave temples in the epoch of the Pallavas of Kāñci.

68 See Ch. 23, Ch. 57, etc.

69 Ch. 244, 25 ff.

70 *Ibid.*, 3 and 5.

The Vāsudeva-cult.

Allied to this is the cult of Vāsudeva.[71] The worship and prayer to Vāsudeva are prescribed by the Matsya Purāṇa. Among the diverse religious modes of worship which were prevalent in ancient India, one that was prominent was the Vāsudeva worship. According to the late R. G. Bhandarkar the Vāsudeva-Kṛṣṇa worship owes its origin to the stream of thought which began with the Upaniṣads and arose about the time of the rise of Jainism and Buddhism. It cannot be disputed that it prevailed in the time of the first Maurya Candragupta.[72] The Vāsudeva cult signifies the rise of the Bhāgavata School. The identification of Vāsudeva with Viṣṇu, the Vedic deity, is seen in the great epic. Bhandarkar holds that this cult began with the Sātvatas and then spread to other tribes and peoples.[73] Be this what it may, the cult can be said to be coeval with the rise of Jainism and Buddhism and hence about the 5th or 6th century B.C. or a little earlier. It is worthy of note that the Matsya Purāṇa does not speak of the cult of Gopālakṛṣṇa of which the Bhāgavata Purāṇa is full.

The Lingāyatana ārādhyas.

The next topic of interest for chronological considerations is the mention of the Lingāyatana ārādhyas. While it is certainly possible to get at the origin of the different religious sects flourishing in ancient times it is difficult to trace the origin of Śaivism. This antique sect had its origin in the prehistoric period, and was

71 Ch. 242, 16.

72 See *Vaiṣṇavism, Śaivism*, etc., p. 9.

73 *Ibid.*

in existence much earlier than the chalcolithic period of ancient India as testified to us by the interesting finds of the Indus valley. It is so ancient that a claim is made that it was non-Aryan religion to begin with. Into the merits of this question we need not go for the present. There can be no two opinions as to the antiquity of that religion. Its votaries worshipped Śiva in the form of an image and in the form of a liṅga, from earliest times. But the latter was the more popular adopted by the masses of the people. As centuries passed and with the widening of culture, a number of branches were seen one after another on the old tree of Śaivism. One such distinguishing branch was the sect of Lingāyatana ārādhyas, which latterly came to be known as the Vīraśaivas. From the epithet Lingāyatana appended to Ārādhyas it is clear that this Śaiva sect of the Ārādhyas were worshippers of the Liṅga, the symbolical representation of Śiva.

It has been observed that the Lingāyats are a very recent sect of the Vīraśaivas who owe their existence to Basava, the Brahman minister of Vijjana, the Kālacūri usurper to the Cāḷūkya throne, and that this Vijjana was assasinated by a Jaṅgama in 1167 A.D. It is said that after him the Lingāyat sect spread in the kingdom of Kuntala or the Southern Maratha country, and was successful in throwing out Jainism from the Karnāṭaka country.[74]

There is today what is known as the Basava Purāṇa which has deified Basava, as an avatār of Nandi, the

74 C. V. Vaidya, *A History of Medieval Hindu India*, Vol. III, pp. 420—421.

Bull of Śiva, the purpose of the incarnation being the re-establishment of the decaying Śaiva religion. This legend need not deter us. What is learnt from it is that Basava was a Brahman of the ārādhya sect who took on himself the role of a religious reformer and introduced certain innovations into the tenets and practices of the ancient religious sect of Ārādhyas, of which he was an honoured member. He interested himself to find out as esoteric meaning of the symbol of *liṅga,* and to make the Liṅgāyats wear it constantly on their person. To his call the mercantile and agricultural classes in Karnāṭaka readily responded, and Vīraśaivism gained in numerical strength.

To our purpose what is significant is that the Ārādhyas are a much older sect of people than one will imagine them to be, and that these Ārādhyas have later on merged into the liṅgāyats otherwise known as Jangamas, after its revival by Basava in the twelfth century A.D. It is worthy to note that the Matsya Purāṇa refers to this sect when it mentions Liṅgāyatana Vipras.[75] This sect must have existed not later than the third century A.D. It also shows that this sect was not entirely a non-Brahmanical sect, as it is generally understood to be. Even today we hear that among the Brahmana community there is a section, though small in numbers, of Vīraśaivas of the Liṅgāyat creed.[76]

75 Ch. 230—4.

लिङ्गायतनविप्रेषु तत्रवासं नरोचयेत् ।

76 See, for example, Rice, *History of Kanarese Literature*, pp. 49—55; also *Mysore Gazetteer*, Vol. I, New Edition, pp. 322 ff.

Ārdhanārīśvara temple.

Among the singular medley of divine figures, in the Rudra-Śiva complex, Ardhanārīśvara appears in the picture. The figure is represented to be of two halves, the right being one part of Rudraśiva and the left being one part of Umā-Gaurī. A critical student of Indian iconography will treat this as only a freak of Indian sculpture and architecture. To a student of Indian philosophy, it has an esoteric meaning. It is a representation of an early symbol of the active and passive aspects of creative power. Commenting on the figure at Elephanta the late archaeologist Burgess remarked that:—

> "such a representation of creative power must be of considerable antiquity, for exactly such a statute as this is mentioned by Porphyry as having been described as Bardesanes of Babylon by the Indian Sandeles and his companions, ambassador in the time of Elagabalus, about A.D. 220; and what is curious they described it as being of ten or twelve cubits in height, in a large cave in a mountain, standing erect, the right side being male from head to foot, the left female, and over the arm's a number of angles, particulars that could only refer to something very like what is actually found here." [77]

This representation is of considerable antiquity not only in Indian folklore but also the folklore of all the ancient world. There are a good many shrines today in India where the deity in half-male and half-female form

77 See also K. H. Vakil, *Rock-cut temples around Bombay*, pp. 50—51.

is worshipped. The Matsya Purāṇa in its reference to this shrine[78] known as kṛtaśauca narrates a legend as to its origin. Briefly told, the mātas or goddesses who were created by Śiva to put down the aśuras gave untold trouble to the Lord that he remembered Nṛsimha who successfully put down their wrath and energy. In honour of this, Śiva in ardhanāri form praised Nṛsimha in that spot and went to his permanent abode. The Hill at Tiruccengode, Salem District in South India, celebrated in the days of the Śangam epoch as a Subrahmaṇya shrine, has for its central shrine Ardhanārīśvara. In the same compound to the north-east there is a Viṣṇu shrine. Whoever goes to worship at this hill cannot miss this Viṣṇu shrine. To venture a conjecture the description of the Purāṇa may be a reference to this sacred ancient hill. As if to corroborate this legend there is the great shrine of Narasimha at Nāmakkal about 20 miles from this Hill. It is a cave temple with a large figure of Narasimha in it. K. P. Jayaswal and Dr. Hira Lal inform me that they are not aware of any temple dedicated to Ardhanārīśvara in North India with a Viṣṇu shrine in the same compound. These pieces of evidence go to confirm what we have ventured to conjecture. Last but not least is the reference to betel leaves.

Conclusion.

To recapitulate the aforesaid examination and conclusions, the date of the Matsya Purāṇa is to be spread over a number of centuries commencing probably with

78 Ch. 179, 87—89.

the third or fourth century B.C. and ending with the third century A.D. This Purāṇa is undoubtedly to be placed in the post-epic and post-Dharmasūtra period. The geneological lists including that of the Kali age do not take us beyond the history of the Andhras and Śakas. The Guptas are not mentioned. From this it is quite clear that the lowest chronological limit cannot be later than 300 A.D. roughly. Though there are certain data which bespeak of a higher antiquity, as we observed in the course of the above survey, still the language and style preclude us from being guided by mere references, some of which might have been accidental. There are no archaic expressions, and the Purāṇa indicates that it is far ahead of the sūtra form of style which was employed by the authors of the Arthaśāstra and the Kāmasūtra. The stanzas are couched in elegant literary style in conformity to the Pāṇinīan standards. Though a few portions may be assigned to pre-Patañjali period, the major portion of it is definitely later than Patañjali. Thus though we cannot definitely fix a period for the upper limit of the age of the Purāṇa, caution requires that we must be moderate in assigning dates for compositions of this kind. It is quite plausible to take the view that the Purāṇa texts are older, but what we are actually concerned today is the probable period during which the Matsya Purāṇa, as we know today, took its shape. To venture a conjecture it may have been reduced to writing in a period not far from that of Patañjali, and it may be that in the dark period of India's history, the period covering the decline of the Andhra power and the rise of the Gupta power, a new redaction was called for, and at that time the redactor added a few portions only in the geneological lists furnished to make it up to date.

According to Pargiter "there is an apparent indication that a compilation was begun in the later part of the second century in the Andhra King, Yajñaśri's reign, for, five mss. of the Matsya Purāṇa (of which three appear to be independent, namely b. c. and i.) speak of him as reigning in his ninth or tenth year".[79] As against this theory, two objections can be raised. One is that the theory is based on the reading—nava varṣāṇi Yajñaśrīḥ kurute śāta karṇikaḥ. But the other reading adopted by the editor of the Poona edition militates against this: nava vimaśati varṣāṇi yajñaśrīḥ śātakarṇikaḥ meaning that the reign of Yajñaśri extended to 29 years. This reading perhaps keeps in with the usual manner in which the list is narrated to us. Even granting for the sake of argument we adopted the first reading which seems to make a specific statement, viz.: the ninth year of Yajñaśri's reign, what answer have we to give for the continuance of the list to the very end of the Andhra dynasty? If we have to take as Pargiter would have it, the Purāṇic list must come to an end with Yajñaśri. The very fact that kings who succeeded Yajñaśri are mentioned shows the reading adopted by the Ānandāśrama edition to be more correct and precise.

The second difficulty is whether the Purāṇa as a whole in its present form was compiled in the second century, or only the dynastic account as

79 See p. xiii the *Dynasties of the Kali Age.*

narrated by the Purāṇa. It appears more logical and more reasonable that in that century or a little later the dynastic portion was brought up to date, for, other portions of the Purāṇa bear an air of antiquity about them. The chapters 271—3 which are tacked on at the end of the Purāṇa follow so closely the Vāyu version that they do not seem to be original. It stands to reason, therefore, that there was the hand of the redactor only with regard to the dynastic account and not to other portions. On this account we can well assign to this Purāṇa a place among the oldest of the Purāṇas.[80] To advert to what we have already said, though the Vāyu Purāṇa refers to the Gupta and other dynasties, and though the Matsya Purāṇa stops short of the Andhra dynasty, still the material of the Vāyu is much older than the Matsya Purāṇa. If by the term 'oldest' is meant only second century A.D. we are not only prepared to grant it but also to go further back by three or four centuries.

80 See in this connection V. A. Smith, *Oxford History of India*, p. 33.

CHAPTER III.

THE POLITY AS DESCRIBED IN THE PURĀṆA.

As we have already seen the Purāṇa contains some interesting chapters on political and administrative institutions. This is not all. Here and there, a student of ancient Indian polity comes across a number of stray references which throw side-lights on the polity of the ancient Hindus. Though the Matsya Purāṇa does not cite Kauṭalya by name, still it mentions the Arthaśāstra in a number of places. The prescriptions laid down for the conduct of the administration in general afford a striking parallel to those of the Kauṭalīya. A close correspondence of the two texts shows that the Purāṇa follows the Kauṭalīya in its recommendation. In the following pages we shall try to study the polity as described in the Matsya Purāṇa and endeavour to show how far the Purāṇa is indebted to the Arthaśāstra of Kauṭalya.

The King.

In ancient Indian polity the King occupied the first place. As a Kṣatriya he should follow the prescribed course of conduct (*brahmavidhi*) which alone would make his position safe and secure (*akṣayavidhi*).[1] His chief duties[2] were (1) to protect his subjects, (2) to show special consideration to Brahmans, the distressed, the infirm, widows and ascetics, (3) to

1 Ch. 215, 58—59.

2 *Ibid.*, 60 ff.

so conduct himself that the subjects would look upon him as a father, (4) to fight without retreating from the field of battle, (5) to perform sacrifices and give gifts without any stint so as to attain spiritual glory, and (6) to patronise learning by propagating the study of the Vedic literature in his kingdom.

The king should further inspire confidence in his neighbours and subjects, keep his weaknesses undivulged and behave like a tortoise in his state policy.[3] He should be nonsectarian in religious policy, tolerant and amiable to all. It is prescribed that the king should protect his person from the undesirables and especially be careful in his private life, when taking his meals, going to bed, decking himself with ornaments and flowers, bathing in unfamiliar places and indulging with unknown women. Again whenever he went out in public, such as to visit a festival, he should go sufficiently guarded lest no harm should befall his person (ch. 215). In a word he should exercise self-restraint.

Palace : The king's residence was to be in a central place well fortified. The fortress was to be surrounded by a ditch and ramparts and well provided with superior weapons, thus making it impossible for the enemy to make an assault. The Purāṇa furnishes us with ideas as to the size of the royal capital, the fortification and its walls, its different roads, residences of officials including those of the judicial and the military

3 *Ibid.*, 67.

departments, the treasury, stables for elephants and horses, the arsenal, store houses, residences of Brahmans and artisans by the side of rivers, fruit and flower gardens, besides all varieties of medicinal plants. A careful storage of different kinds of poisons is recommended with a view to counteract the machinations of the enemy to bring about their destruction.[3a]

Six varieties of fortresses are distinguished.[3b] Each was a storehouse of medicines of all sorts. The object was, first, to get rid of the demons, and secondly, to dispel the effect of poisons. The medicines in the nature of decoctions which would afford interesting and valuable material to a student of Āyurveda, made of rare herbs and roots, show how people were fully superstitious, afraid of poisons and demons in those days. In fact we are made to believe that the kingship in ancient India glibly termed autocratic by modern scholars, was not a bed of roses. The prescriptions like the following that cooked food should be tested by fire or some other method, and that clothes, flowers, and ornaments should be examined before use, show that the sovereign lived in an atmosphere of suspicion and doubted very much the loyalty of his servants. These are only few among many evidences. The implication is, as has been expressed elsewhere,[3c] that ancient Indian governments being largely monarchical in character depended, to a large extent, on the dominating personality of the sovereign.

3a For other details the reader's attention is drawn to chapter 217.

3b See Ch. 218.

3c See my *Mauryan Polity*, p. 72 and 73.

The place of the king in the constitution: The importance of the sovereign in the ancient Hindu polity can be well realised from the first place assigned to him among the seven elements of sovereignty which constituted the state in ancient India. It must be remembered that this importance assigned to the sovereign did not mean that he was the All-Powerful Mighty Lord, a dictator whose word was law and a despot to whom the subjects obeyed in servility. Far from that. In the days with which we are now concerned men believed, superstitiously as we would say, that the Gods walked on the earth, and that one such God was the king himself. This theocratic idea invested the person of the king with a halo of sacredness and invoked regard and respect even from the intellegentia, not to speak of the masses. This is exactly the feeling of the Purāṇa writer when he says that a king is a creation of Brahmā, that he resembles the Sun God and the Moon in his looks, Dharmarāja (deity of death) in bestowing affection and inflicting punishment, the God Varuṇa to his enemy and Indra in sustaining his subjects.[4]

The theory of Divine Right: The king is again Agni, Vāyu, and Pṛthvī.[5] In fact the attributes of every Vedic deity are bestowed on the monarch. It was not the divine hereditary right which James I and his allies claimed in the 17th century, and which Louis XIV of France put into practice with his favourite maxim *L'etat c' est moi* (I am the state). Human nature being what it is, unless there is the fear of the royal rod

4 Cp. *Manu*, VII, 3 & 4.

5 Ch. 226.

of punishment, people would be prone to commit heinous offences with the result that there would be neither peace nor progress, if things were allowed to take their own course. According to the ancient political concept everything is made to rest on daṇḍa.[6]

The King, the moral Custodian: Thus the sovereign of the land was primarily looked upon as the moral custodian of the state. As has been already said, it was an age of rank superstition. People believed in the ominous signs, both in the celestial and terrestrial regions, as foreboding some evil to the kingdom. These signs, there were lucky ones also, the king is asked to watch and get them remedied by peace offerings (*śānti*). It is interesting to note that these propitious rites are likened to an armour protecting the warrior from a volley of arrows.[7] A number of śāntis are mentioned in accordance with the nature of the omen, the season and the place of its occurrence. It is natural that there were interpreters of these signs and the śānti was performed according to the construction placed on the respective omens. Generally these ceremonies were conducted in honour of the Vedic deities like the sun, the moon, the wind etc.[8] Among the evil portents one is the falling down of a portion of the palace like the gateway or balcony which is said to forebode the imminent death of the reigning king.[9] Besides the special

6 On the concept of daṇḍanīti see my *Hindu Administrative Institutions*, Ch. 1, Sec. 1.

7 Ch. 228.

8 Ch. 233.

9 Ch. 238, 1.

sacrifices, the king is enjoined to perform Bṛhatyajña, Lakṣahoma and Koṭihoma which would, according to the belief of the times, go a long way to avert the impending evils to his kingdom, or at least to mitigate the rigour of such evils.[10]

The King, a creature of the age: Closely connected with this is the importance and value attached to dreams auspicious or inauspicious especially by a king. The old Greek and Roman conception was that the dream was a warning from God against coming events. Much nearer home we hear of the table of dreams, Tabir Nāma of the Persians. There are in this Purāṇa certain chapters[11] devoted to different dreams and how they are to be interpreted, recalling to our minds the five books of the *Oneirocritica* of Artemidorous who drew his materials from a work on dreams in the library of Aśśur-banipal at Nineveh.[11a] In short the king was a creature of the ideas and theories of the age. It is said elsewhere that the king is the maker of time (kāla). According as the monarch who was at the helm of the affairs of state conducted himself, time was reckoned as kṛta, treta, dvāpara and kali.

The King, a constitutional monarch: It seems that that form of democracy consisting of countless parties deciding questions of state on the strength of a majority vote was discountenanced. It was then realised that a healthy form of monarchy with democratic institutions

10 Ch. 239. Faith in the efficacy of such *homas* is still current in India.

11 Ch. 242.

11a *Ency., of Religion and Ethics,* Vol. V, p. 34.

serving as a check to curb the autocracy of a monarch if he would so behave, was the best form of Government which ensured the progress of the kingdom at large. In pure democracy as it is understood today, we have leaders of parties whose words are respected and adhered to by the respective parties. So also the kings were in early governments leaders of groups composed of all communities whose weal or woe he shared. We can quote here Gierki with profit. He says: "Lordship therefore was never mere right; primarily it was duty."[12] Thus the king was a constitutional monarch, who had no power to make laws, but one who executed the laws already made for him (Dharmaśāstras) often in consultation with a council of the learned.[13]

The king, no autocrat: The king was not free to do as he liked. He would not go against the prescriptions laid down in the codes of law and polity (Dharmaśāstra and Arthaśāstra).[14] If he did, he reaped the consequences thereof. The people disowned him and a state of arājaka set in with all the evils akin to a state of mātsyanyāya.[15]

We have heard of very few cases where kings so misbehaved and got into trouble. Generally the application of daṇḍa was on proper lines with a thorough-going discrimination so much so that people looked upon kings as their fathers and brothers. This is the much

12 Gierki and Maitland: *Political Theories of the Middle Age*, p. 34.

13 227, 217.

14 Ch. 225, 7.

15 See *Hindu Ad. Institutions*, Ch. 1, Sec. 3.

misunderstood paternal conception of the Hindu monarchy.

Daṇḍa: In this connection we can refer to the concept of daṇḍanīti as promulgated by the Matsya Purāṇa. Daṇḍa is elevated to the rank of the different expedients which the king should resort to according to the circumstances. The Purāṇa gives a categorical list of these expedients which are seven in number. These are[16]—

Sāma,
bheda,
dāna,
daṇḍa,
Upekṣā,
Māyā and
Indrajāla.

According to the Arthaśāstra texts and the epics, the first four are the recognised traditional expedients. They were, in truth, the chief diplomatic methods in ancient India. The Purāṇa accepts the traditional classification and adds three more, an evidence of the advance in that science and a testimony to mark the work as a post-epic composition. It has been often remarked that in ancient India one could not trace a history of political thought, and that political science remained stagnant. This is far from the truth. This is not the place to examine the pros and cons of this all important question. Suffice it to say, that the roots of

16 Ch. 222.

political science as can be gleaned from the Vedic sources sprouted into a plant in the days of the Dharma-sūtras, and grew into a tree in the epoch of the Artha-śāstra. From that time onward the tree may be said to have been growing with its various branches overladen with fruits and flowers. The Matsya Purāṇa envisages some such period. In the Arthaśāstra of Kauṭalya we do not hear of these seven expedients.

The Purāṇa speaks of a two-fold classification of Sāma—the satya sāma and the asatya sāma, genuine or otherwise.[17] The theory of the Purāṇa is that people in the world are either righteous or unrighteous. So application of policy must differ from person to person. Satya sāma must be used towards the righteous and asatya sāma must be used towards the unrighteous. By appealing to the ancientness of his family and by appreciating with approval the deeds done by certain righteous persons one was easily reconciled. This is characterised as satya-sāma. If such a policy of reconcilation was pursued in the case of the wicked, it dangerously affected the king's position. For the wicked would be apt to think in their foolishness that the king was afraid of them and would indulge in more mischief.[18] So a wise king is asked to pursue the policy of dissension (*bheda*) towards the wicked. This is nothing more than the policy of 'divide and rule'. An empire, according to the Purāṇa, is liable to two chief sources of danger—internal and

17 For more sub-divisions see the *Śivatatvaratnākara* of the 17th century, 5. 12. 50 ff.

18 Ch. 222.

external. By the policy of *bheda* the king is advised to get rid of the internal dissensions. For without peace at home it would not be possible to launch a policy of aggression. To conquer an enemy is to create a division among his kinsmen and to attack him when they would be disunited.

The third is the policy of dāna or gifts. It is said that even the gods are brought round through gifts. This is commended as the best expedient to win over the recalcitrant and the rebellious. But there might be people who would not be won over by these three expedients, and to them daṇḍa is recommended. The application of daṇḍa must be wise and just. To that effect the king must consult his councillors and act according to the injunctions of the established law-codes.[19] As an expedient in foreign politics daṇḍa means launching a policy of open war, other diplomatic means failing. In this connection a reference may be made to the chapter[20] where the discussion centres round the question when and how a king should march for war. One's own kingdom is said to be the base of all operations. Therefore when a king finds peace prevailing in his kingdom, and the enemy in adverse circumstances in some form or other, he can well begin his expedition. Different seasons suit different limbs of the army but the vernal season suits all the fourfold forces. Approximate to the religious standards of the

19 संयक्प्रणयनंतस्य तथा कार्यं महीक्षिता ।
धर्मशास्त्रानुसारेण सुसहायेन धीमता ॥ Ch. 225—2.

20 Ch. 240.

age in which the Purāṇa was compiled, there is the injunction that on the eve of the march the king should note the auspicious and inauspicious omens, on which, it was believed, depended victory or defeat.[21] But if the conquering monarch be more powerful it would be shortsighted policy for a less powerful sovereign to attack him. To such weak kings, the Purāṇa recommends three more expedients—upekṣā, māyā, and indrajāla.

Upekṣā, māyā and indrajāla : Let us now examine the significance of these modes of policy recommended by the Matsya Purāṇa. By adding Upekṣā after daṇḍa the Purāṇa seems to imply that a weak king should play the part of a neutral, or in other words should be indifferent. There seems to be the further implication that even in case the more powerful king gives trouble, the small king is advised to endure it for the time being until he feels sufficiently strong to lead an expedition. To a king who does not possess the powers of endurance it would appear that the policy of māyā or indrajāla is recommended. Māyā is a baser kind of diplomacy and the king who would pursue it, should resort to cunning and intriguing methods. He should discard the straight path and try his best to hoodwink the enemy by a recourse to the expedient māyā. The next expedient mentioned is indrajāla that partakes of the nature and character of māyā. This is the use of strategem in war. It would appear that these methods were not used in battles of a *dharmavijaya*

21 Ch. 241.

nature but only in *āsura and lobha vijayas* which are not commended by any law-giver and which run against the accepted ethics of warfare in ancient India. The mere mention by an Arthaśāstra writer who is out to discuss the pros and cons of a question cannot and should not be mistaken to be a recommendation of the writer, or his view of a particular question or a series of questions. By a study of ancient Indian political thought in this light the so-called Machiavellian character of the recommendations of our ancient authors of polity vanish into thin air.

The Council.

As we have already remarked, the polity as expounded by the Matsya Purāṇa envisages a system of constitutional monarchy. The continuity of kingship was assured because of its reconciliation with democracy. In the interests of discipline and progress it was regarded not only as a useful but also an essential institution. As the executive head, the crown enjoyed all powers but could not but respect convention and usage. In this respect the ancient Indian Government may be said to resemble the modern English constitution in which the king is by law the executive head while the real governing body is the cabinet. What part the cabinet plays to-day the royal council fulfilled in ancient times in India with one little difference. While the cabinet is responsible to the Parliament in the theory of English constitution, the council in ancient India was responsible both to the king and the people. The paramount importance attached to this institution by Kauṭalya is clear from the deliberate statement that all kinds of administrative business are preceded by deliberations in a well-formed council.[22] This view is abundantly shared by the Matsya Purāṇa when it says that the king should consult his council of ministry and take its advice and finally make up his mind with regard to the affairs of state. For, the Purāṇa is explicit when it states that the prosperity of the kingdom depends solely on the men in council.[23]

The members constituting this body were to be highly competent and at the same time respectable. The qualifications expected of each of the members are high and speak to the credit of an efficient system of administration conducted on sound lines.[24] The Matsya Purāṇa seems to propound the theory that on the council lies the basis of sound policy, and hence the members chosen should be men of genuine ability and of good character. As regards the composition and procedure of the council, it is said that the king should neither hold council with one minister nor with too many.[25] In awarding punishments apparently in cases

22 I. 15.

23 Ch. 215, 2, 3.

अभिषेकार्द्रशिरसा राज्ञा राज्यावलोकिना ।
सहायवरणंकार्यँ तत्रराज्यं प्रतिष्ठितम् ॥
यदप्यल्पतरं कर्म तदप्येकेनदुष्करम् ।
पुरुषेणासहायेन किमुराज्यंमहोदयम् ॥

24 Ibid 4—7 and 24.

25 Cp. *Arthaśāstra*, Bk. I, Sec. 15; *Matsya Purāṇa* 220, 33—36.

relating to appeal, the king is advised to hold consultation with the learned.[26] In the matter of consultation the prescription agrees again with that of the Kauṭalīya and the epics. Whenever a consultation is held, the king is advised to consult his councillors individually and then jointly. The idea was that there should not be even the slightest confusion in matters of administrative importance. Ultimate decision rested upon the advice of the prime minister who was supposed to give expert advice.[27]

Thus the institution of council constituted a great check on the king's prerogative. Though similar institutions existed in the early Government of the Greeks, kingship did not become rooted in ancient Greece. The fact was that the council of elders was dominated in ancient Greece by the aristocrats who paved the way for the disruption of monarchy and for the rise of their own power. This is due to the disproportion of the different parts of the polity. Ancient Indian polity was however conceived on entirely different lines, conformable in some respects to the Aristotelean polity, where 'all the parts of the polity are mingled in proper proportions.'[28]

Other institutions.

A number of political and administrative institutions appropriate to a monarchical Government are

26 227—217.

27 215, 46—49.

28 R. H. Murray: *The History of Political Science*, p. 28.

mentioned in the Matsya Purāṇa.[28a] Apart from the personal attendants on the king like the personal guards, the door-keepers, the betel bearers, the physician and the cook, there were other servants of the Government, who were appointed to the respective departments, after having been properly tested as to their ability and honesty. In the military department there was the Commander-in-chief who might be a Brahmana or a Kṣatriya, the minister of war versed in Ṣaḍanga or sixfold policy of sandhi, vigraha, yāna, āsana, dvaidhībhāva and āśraya and also versed in the different languages of the country, the men in charge of the four-fold forces, the controller of the arsenal, and skilled spies.

A word may be said about the institution of spies. Its value to other departments was equally recognised. There was an elaborate spy system and it seems to have been an accepted principle of Hindu administrations that secret spies should be sent out to the different parts of the kingdom's as well as to foreign countries to get an intimate knowledge of the peoples' minds and the movements of the enemy kings. However the King was not to place implicit faith in the version of any one spy, but must take action if the statement of one spy was corroborated by that of the others.[29] The Purāṇa recommends the sending of four spies apparently for a single purpose, in the guise of merchants, astrologers, sannyāsins and physicians. The Kauṭalīya

28a For the existence of the Paura and Jānapada assemblies see above p. 63.

29 cp. *Arthaśāstra*, Bk. I, Sec. 12.

says that the spies are the eyes of the king. The Purāṇa further follows the Arthaśāstra in its recommendations of setting up spies over different departments of the state to watch the conduct of the Government servants. The spy chosen was to be a linguist and a good speaker according to the conditions and circumstances of the time and the place. Generally the trustworthy servants of the state were sent out in the disguise of ascetics.

The next important department that demands our attention is the finance department. There was the king's treasurer who was above avarice and had ability to gauge the value of things. The chief articles that went into the treasuries were iron, cloth, deer-skin, and jewels. The superintendent of the treasury had a number of assistants. There was an officer in charge of disbursements and his status was equal to that of the treasurer. He in his turn had his own assistants. The accountants who were in charge of accounts were men who could write neatly and legibly, who were educated and clever enough to use short phrases full of pregnant sense and meaning. It was further the function of the department to see that the money was spent on useful and productive purposes.[30]

There was, again, the department of justice, where skilled men and experts in law-codes were appointed as Judges. There is a long and very interesting chapter[31] containing 217 stanzas dealing with offences, their nature and the punishment prescribed for each. Some

30 Ch. 220, 12—13.

31 227.

of the offences are misappropriation of things placed under custody, illegal sale of property, infringement of promise, misbehaviour with married and unmarried girls, violation of the chastity of women, destruction of forests, gardens and fields, the killing of men and animals like the cow, straying away from the prescribed path of conduct; theft, withholding wages or neglecting to complete the work undertaken, speaking falsehood, misbehaving with prostitutes, misappropriation of revenues by the officials of the state, practice of vaśīkaraṇam and ābhicāra rites, eating forbidden things, etc. To these a number of *prāyaścittas* like kṛcchra or ardhakṛcchra are ordained for purification. There were again offences which could be mitigated by fines. Yet were others where mutilation of particular limbs or killing of the offender is recommended. The punishments seem to have been very severe and rigid in character. In these injunctions the Matsya Purāṇa largely follows the *Mānava Dharma śāstra* and the *Arthaśāstra* as well. In recommending such severity of punishments it would appear that the state struck terror into the minds of the people which went a long way to minimise crimes. In fact crimes were then few and far between. In prescribing that the fallen mother should not be abandoned, and that the Brahman guilty of crime should be banished and not condemned to death, the Purāṇa follows completely the injunction of the *Arthaśāstra*. Last but not least was the department of the seraglio where aged and respectable men were placed in charge.[32]

32 See Ch. 215.

There is an excellent chapter[33] on the conduct of Government servants reminding us of the section *upayukta* of the *Arthaśāstra.*[34] It would not be out of place to summarise this chapter as it concerns every servant of the state at all times and in all places. A Government servant must be loyal, faithful, and true to his word. In the public he must speak words agreeable to the king and not cross him. If he would feel that the king was absolutely going wrong in a manner prejudicial to his own well-being, then, he must seek audience in private and speak to him what he felt with regard to that particular matter. Two things are to be clearly avoided—overwork and misappropriation. The Government servant must not try to imitate the sovereign in his dress or in speech or such like action. He should show respect to whatever honours are conferred upon him. He must not frequent the harem and other departments intended for royal ladies. Nor should he associate with the spies of the enemy. One should volunteer to do service in the interests of administration but always within the limits of prescribed hours of business. In the assemblage, it is ordained, that Government servants ought not to seat themselves either in front or behind the sovereign, but only on either side of the king's seat. The Government servant is expected to conduct himself in a manner which would not cost him his appointment, but which would lead to his general welfare. Thus only he would earn the goodwill of the state authorities and increase his own

33 Ch. 216.

34 Bk. II, Ch. 9.

interests. For it is prescribed that, to begin with, they must be started on a low scale and must be promoted to a higher scale gradually if they gave full satisfaction.[35]

The Crown Prince.

There were again regulations regarding the king's conduct towards the Prince Royal.[35a] He must be well guarded by means of a good number of reliable servants. A trustworthy tutor must be appointed to train him in the right direction. Chief attention was paid to instructing him in physical culture to make him an able warrior. There is a curious prescription of the Matsya Purāṇa that the prince need not rigorously speak the truth always but speak sweet words as the exigencies of the occasion required. It is rather difficult to realise the full implication of this aspect of instruction to a prince. Probably the exigencies of the state demanded it. If he was trained to speak nothing but the bare truth, sometimes, such true words would be displeasing to others, and that his career would have to begin with the prejudice and ill will of a discontented section. Otherwise this injunction is neither sound nor valid. As a prince it was just possible that his mind was poisoned by interested people with all sorts of temptations. So it is said that his personal guards should be such as would

35 220, 7.

अधिकारेषुसर्वेषु विनीतं विनियोजयेत् ।
आदौ स्वल्पे ततः पश्चात्क्रम क्रमेणाथ महत्स्वपि ॥

35a See in this connection my *Hindu Administrative Institutions*, Ch. III, Sec. 1.

wean him away from baneful and bad influences. Much stress is laid upon his environment. He should be ever surrounded by good and virtuous persons, who, by precept and by example, would make him walk in the path of virtue. If, in spite of such precautionary measures, a prince proved refractory and seemed to err from the righteous walk of life, he was confined to some secret but well guarded place. That prince, who was devoid of statesmanship and the virtue of humility, would not thrive. Hence the Matsya Purāṇa insists on a proper and rigid course of instruction which would stand the prince in good stead when he would take up the reins of government into his own hands.[36]

Nor is this all. The prince was kept away from such vices as drinking, hunting, and gambling. For there are many instances where kings had gone to ruin by overindulgence in some of these vices. Another healthy restriction is that the prince was prevented from sleeping during day time and also from going on tour with no specific purpose in view. Such things, it need not be said, would go a long way in cultivating the habit of Utthāna much insisted on for a king by all the *nīti* literature.[37] For in the succeeding chapter[38] there is a discussion as to which is superior, fate or one's own exertion and effort, and it is concluded that exertion and effort are superior to fate, for, by perseverance even fate would be conquered, a statement recalling to our

36 See Ch. 220, 1—6.

37 Ibid. 8—9. Cp. Ar. Śās. Bk. I, Ch. 19; and Bk. VI, Ch. 1.

38 221.

mind the beautiful maxim of the sacred Kuṟaḷ[39] to the same effect. The Purāṇa in fact condemns him who stakes his all on fate and is not active and alert.

The foregoing examination shows that the polity, of the Purāṇa bears, except in certain details, close resemblance to the Kauṭalīyan polity. Tradition has built up the edifice of ancient Indian political science on the bedrock of *saptāṅga* and this the Purāṇa accepts when it speaks of the ministers, subjects, forts, army, treasury and ally[40] together with the king, forming the seven component parts of an empire,[41] and also when it insists on the king protecting all these limbs of the state.

Lastly, there is the question of the sixteen *mahādānas* which a monarch is asked to perform on particular occasions. It is not certainly restricted to the king[41a] but is enjoined as a charity to any wealthy and learned man. This institution can be traced back to the *pratigraha mantra* section of the Taittirīya Brāhmaṇa II. 3. 4; and the Taittirīya Āraṇyaka fur-

39 cp. the *Kuṟal.*

தெய்வத்தா னாகாதெனினு முயற்சிதன்
மெய் வருத்தக் கூலிதரும் (619)

ஊழையு முப்பக்கங் காண்ப ருலைவின்றித்
தாழா துஞற்று பவர். (620)

40 Three kinds of allies are mentioned—hereditary friends, enemies' enemy, and a friend acquired out of necessity.

41 Ch. 220, 19.

41a The Liṅga Purāṇa speaks of *Rājñāmṣoḍaśadānāni*, *Uttara*, Ch. 28-14.

nishes a list of 17 dānas[41b] of which some come under the category of the gifts referred to in the Purāṇa. According to the latter they are as follows:

i. Tulā puruṣa dāna—or a gift equal to the weight of a man in gold. This is said to be the first and best of all gifts.[42]

ii. Hiraṇyagarbha dāna—a gift of a golden vessel called hemagarbha.[43]

iii. Brahmāṇḍa dāna or a mundane egg to be made and worshipped on an auspicious day and given away as a gift.[44]

iv. Kalpapādapa dāna—a gift of a tree of paradise. This is said to be equal in merit to the Aśvamedha sacrifice.[45]

v. Gosahasraka dāna—gift of thousand cows.[46]

vi. Hiraṇya kāmadhenu dāna—a gift of a celestial cow of gold.[47]

41b. अग्नये हिरण्यम्.....

सोमाय वासः रुद्राय गाम् वरुणायाश्वं प्रजापतये पुरुषं मनवे तल्पं। त्वष्ट्रेऽजाम्। पूष्णेऽविम्। निऋत्या अश्वतरगर्दभौ हिमवतो हस्तिनम्। गन्धर्वाप्सराभ्यः स्रगलंकरणे। विश्वेभ्योदेवेभ्यो धान्यम्। वाचेऽन्नम् ब्रह्मण ओदनम्। समुद्रायापः उत्तानायाऽङ्गीरसायानः। वैश्वानराय रथम्। III. 10.

42 For details see Ch. 274.

43 „ 275.

44 „ 276.

45 „ 277.

46 „ 278.

47 „ 279.

vii. Hiraṇyāśvadāna—or a gift of a horse of gold. This is said to confer numberless benefits on the devotee.[48]

viii. Hiraṇyāśvaratha dāna—a gift of a horse chariot of gold. The giver is said to attain beatitude after being freed from all sins.[49]

ix. Hemahastiratha dāna—a gift of an elephant car of gold.[50]

x. Pañca lāṅgalabhū dāna—a gift of a plot of land measuring five ploughs.[51]

xi. Dharā dāna—a gift of an earth of gold in imitation of Jambūdvīpa.[52]

xii. Viśvacakra dāna—a gift of a wheel of the universe weighing from 1000 *palas* of gold to 20 *palas* according to the ability of the devotee.[53]

xiii. Mahā Kalpalatā dāna—a gift of a creeper of paradise. Here the worship of devīs and of Lokapālas is inculcated.[54]

xiv. Saptasāgaraka dāna—or a gift of the seven oceans. The ceremonies are performed in

48 For details see Cr. 280.
49 " 281.
50 " 282.
51 " 283.
52 " 284.
53 " 285.
54 " 286.

seven sacrificial pits filled with honey, butter-milk, etc., representing the oceans respectively.[55]

xv. Ratnadhenu dāna—a gift of a jewelled cow.[56]

xvi. Mahābhūtaghaṭa dāna—a gift of a pot containing the five elements.[57]

These dānas or gifts, which are explained in extenso in sixteen separate chapters, are said to have been performed by eminent personages and kings like Kṛṣṇa Vāsudēva, Ambarīṣa, Prahlāda, Pṛthu and Bharata.[58] The object is claimed to be the removal of all ills and difficulties pertaining to the individual and the state. These gifts were believed to prevent difficulties which would otherwise overcome the kingdom as they invoked the aid of gods. They are regarded to be most auspicious, sacred and mysterious. The Purāṇa adds that lucky persons who perform such virtuous deeds live long in peace and ever protected by the devas.[59]

These dānas were continued to be performed by the Hindu kings till a very late period of Indian history. It is of considerable interest and certainly important to note in this connection that we have the valuable testi-

55 For details see Ch. 287.

56 " 288.

57 " 289.

58 Ch. 274, 11—12.

59 See in this connection the Linga Purāṇa, Uttarārdha, where there is a reference to the sixteen Mahādānas in sixteen Chapters 28—44. The following is the name of these dānas: Tulāpuruṣa, hiraṇyagarbha, tilaparvata, svarṇamedini, kalpapādapa, Gaṇaśeśam, suvarṇadhenu, Lakṣmīvṛṣadānam, Gajadānam, Lokapālāṣṭaka dānam, and Brahma-Viṣṇu-Maheśamūrti pradānam.

mony of epigraphy to show that the kings of Vijayanagara actually performed these mahādānas at different centres of pilgrimage and thus endeared themselves to men and gods. Apart from showing that these kings observed and strictly performed orthodox and traditional rituals and ceremonials, it is of significance to remember that these institutions of the Purāṇa were not merely theoretical in character but were put to actual practice by the reigning sovereigns of the land from time to time. One is interested to learn that even today some of these dānas are current in Hindu states like Travancore and the Maharāja gives such gifts on different occasions. Its practice in medieval times is borne out by a number of inscriptions belonging to the epoch of Vijayanagar. From the Udayambākam grant of Kṛṣṇadevarāya (Śaka 1450) it is clear that Vira-narasimha, the elder brother of Kṛṣṇadeva, and the ruler preceding him, actually performed these *mahādānas* at different centres of pilgrimage.[60] That the great Kṛṣṇadeva himself followed his predecessors in this respect is evident from the Hampe inscription of Kṛṣṇadevarāya.[61] The following epigraph neatly gives in a succinct way the sixteen dānas, though in a slightly different order, from that furnished by the Purāṇa:

ब्रह्माण्डं विश्वचक्रं घटमुदितमहाभूतकं रत्नधेनुं
ससांभोधिंच कल्पक्षितिरुहलतिके कांचनीं कामधेनुं ॥
स्वर्णक्ष्मां यो हिरण्याश्वरथमपि तुलापूरुषं गोसहस्रं
हेमाश्वं हेमगर्भं कनककरिरथं पंचलांगल्यतानीत् ॥ V. 18.

60 See *Ep. Ind.*, Vol. XIV, p. 171 f.

61 *Ibid.* Vol. 1, p. 364.

The inscription enumerates the places where these gifts were given and these are—Cidambaram, Pampāpati, Kāḷahasti, Venkaṭādri, Kāñcī, Śrīśaila (Karnul District) Śoṇaśaila (Tiruvaṇṇāmalai), Harihara Kṣetra (on the frontier of Dhārwad), Ahobala, (Karnul District), Saṁgama (Rameśvara ?), Śrīraṅga, Kumbhaghoṇa, Mahānandi (Karnul District), Nivṛtti, Gokarṇa and Rameśvaram.[62] It would appear that these great gifts were not given once in a lifetime but continued to be repeated by a king, 'thus making superfluous his previously acquired great fame'. The Hampe inscription attests[63] that Kṛṣṇarāya gave again and again, for the sake of the supreme happiness, the sixteen gifts according to the prescriptions laid down in the holy books at different centres famous for temples or bathing places. Thus to a student of history the epigraphical confirmation of the Purāṇic statement is indeed valuable.

62 See also Hultzsch, *S. Ind. Inscription*, Vol. I, p. 83 for a similar list of holy places found in copper-plate grant from Śriperumbudur.

63 *Ep. Ind.* I, p. 364, St. 24.

CHAPTER IV.

ARCHITECTURE IN THE MATSYA PURĀṆA.

By far the most interesting and perhaps the most important section of the Matsya Purāṇa is the section relating to architecture and iconography.

Origin.

Before we proceed to examine the vast and varied styles of architecture that are described by this Purāṇa it is of absorbing interest to the historian to trace its origin in ancient India. Students of anthropology do not cease to emphasise that the evolution of original man was from the nomad stage into that of a hunter, then from a cave man to the civilised man. The Brahmāṇḍa Purāṇa traces in almost a similar way the origin and evolution of man from the earliest times. These data enable us indirectly to arrive at the origin of Indian architecture otherwise shrouded in mystery. The following is a summary account of the origin as furnished by the Brahmāṇḍa Purāṇa.[1]

Towards the end of the Kṛta Yuga and the commencement of the Tretā Yuga great changes set in. In the epoch that preceded this, people lived in an ideal state of nature. But after the *sandhi* of the Kṛta yuga, to speak in the language of the Purāṇa, people who used trees as their abodes—for how

1 Ch. 7, 75—6.

long we are unable to gauge—felt the necessity to abandon them for better housing. To the early man the trees furnished food as well as bed and even clothing if he had any. Besides the fruits and the flowers which the trees yielded in the shape of food to the primitive man, they gave him honey to drink. The thick and leafy branches of the lofty trees served him as his place of residence for rest and sleep. But with the commencement of the Tretā Yuga a change crept in. Man found the trees yielding little or no honey. The clouds began to pour rain and the sun's rays pierced into his leafy residence. Nature compelled him to clothe himself and find better shelter from heat and cold. So the early man sought shelter in the caves of mountains where he discovered that neither rain nor sun troubled him. It cannot be said with any definiteness when man took to cave life or when he abandoned it. But the Record of the rocks will tell us that thousands of years passed before the cave man built his own house and took to a village or town life. Surely an epoch set in when the early man became disgusted with cave life and hankered after a more civilised form of dwelling. Born and bred up in the environment of nature and hence imaginative in outlook, the trees which were his original abode, furnished him with the mode on which to build a house.[2] He found the branches of the trees going

[2] प्राद्‌ुर्बभूवुस्तेषां तु वृक्षास्ते गृहसंज्ञिताः ।
वस्त्राणि च प्रसूयंते फलान्याभरणानिच ॥ 7·85.
तथैव जायते तेषां गंधवर्णाणां रसान्वितं
आन्वीषिकं महावीर्यं पुटके पुटकेमधु ॥

lengthwise, breadthwise and crosswise, some shooting out upwards and others bending down by sheer weight. Imagination dictated him to cut down these branches and put them on the ground lengthwise, crosswise, breadthwise, up and down, and thatch them perhaps with the thick leaves. As he did this building mainly by means of branches of trees (śākhās) he named it *śālas.* The parṇaśālas or lofts referred to in ancient Sanskrit works, where sages and seers are said to have performed penance and prayers are characteristic of this stage in the story of the evolution of Indian architecture. The rustic śāla grew into *gṛha* or well-built house which, in course of time, developed into *prāsāda*

तेन वा वर्त्तयंति स्म मुखे त्रेतायुगस्य वै ।
तस्यामेवाल्पशिष्टायां सिद्धयां कालवशात्तदा ।
मधुधुन्वसुनीष्टेषु पर्वतेषु नदीषुच ।
संश्रयंतिच दुर्गाणि धन्वपार्वतमौदकम् ॥
आरब्धास्तान्निकेतान्वै कर्तुंशीतोष्णवारणात् ।
ततस्तान्निर्मयामासुः खटानिचपुराणिच ॥ *Ibid.* 93.
तथा ते पूर्वमासंश्च वृक्षास्तु गृहसंथिताः ।
तथाकर्तुं समारब्धाश्चिंतयित्वा पुनःपुनः ॥
वृक्षस्यावर्ग्गताः शाखा इतश्चैवापरा गताः ।
अथ ऊर्द्धं गताश्चान्या एवं तिर्यग्गताः पराः ॥
बुद्धयान्विष्य यथान्यायं वृक्षशाखा गतायथा ।
यथाकृतास्तुतैःशाखा स्तस्माच्छालास्तुताः स्मृताः॥
एवं प्रसिद्धः शाखाभ्यः शालाश्चैव गृहाणिच
तस्मात्ताश्च स्मृताः शालाः शालात्वंतासुतत्स्मृतम्॥ *Ibid.* 117-20

as it was well built, well furnished, and as it afforded all sorts of convenience.

Though the early man learnt a lesson from the tree and built places of residence, yet he could not find a way to solve the problem of food. The trees no more yielded him enough to eat and drink. In fact he found them growing in diminution and getting dwarfed, as time passed by. To his wonder and surprise there was a heavy downpour and immediately after it he found plants shooting forth on soil that was unsown and unploughed. He experimented on these and discovered fourteen kinds of grains, all eatables.[3] Thus the tale of evolution goes on and we have to stop here as it no more pertains to the subject on hand.

Thus we have a stimulating account of the origin of house building in ancient India which gradually led to the settlement of villages and towns according as the number of people increased. With these introductory remarks we shall proceed to examine the materials contained in the several chapters of the Matsya Purāṇa. At the outset, one thing is clear, viz.: this Purāṇa envisages a period of great advancement in that science. We are no more in the world of crude architecture when man's knowledge was confined to the use of wood. Here is an age in which the use of stone had already become

[3] अपां भूमेस्तु संयोगादोषध्यस्तास्तदाभवत् ।
पुष्पमूलफलिन्यस्तु ओषध्यस्ता हि ज्ञहिरे ॥
अफालकृष्टाश्चानुप्ता ग्राम्यारण्याश्चतुर्दश ।
कतुपुष्पफलाश्चैव वृक्षा गुल्माश्च जहिरे ॥ *Ibid.* 126-7.

ancient. Though stone was the chief material for building yet wood was also in use. Thus a study of the material assists in building up, by comparison, with data furnished by other works of art and literature, rigid chronological sequences.

Authors of the Science.

The Matsya Purāṇa mentions as many as eighteen teachers of Vāstu Śāstra.[4] These are Bhṛgu, Atri, Vasiṣṭha, Viśvakarmā, Maya, Nārada, Nagnajit, Viśālākṣa, Indra, Brahmā, Svāmikārtika, Nandīśvara, Śaunaka, Garga, Kṛṣṇa, Aniruddha, Śukra, and Bṛhaspati. Though most of these may be mythological names still it is reasonable to presume that some of them were historical personages and were celebrated authors on the science of architecture.

Vāstudeva.

As is common with everything in ancient India, things secular were not divorced from things religious. Though architecture was a secular science, still there was the vāstudeva, the presiding deity of all buildings. The legendary origin of this deva as springing from the sweat of Śiva need not detain us here.[5] Whatever this may be, the fact was that all building commenced according to rules with the worship of this Vāstudeva. This custom has not yet died out in this country. Our masons and carpenters

4 Ch. 252, 2 ff.

5 *Ibid.* See also the 7th Chapter of *Śilparatna* of the 16th Century. (Triv. Sans. Series).

begin their work after offering due prayers to this deity.

Vāstumaṇḍalam.

The building was always started at an auspicious time already chosen for the purpose, in which, the month, the asterism', the week day, the *muhūrta* and the *lagna* were taken into careful consideration. It is believed that only certain months, certain asterisms, and certain days are beneficial, and not all.[6] Then came the examination of the soil by the process of digging the earth. There were other means by which the land was also tested.[7] The whole building was planned and named Vāstumaṇḍalam. The Purāṇa gives a measurement of a house of 64 feet[8] and of 81 feet.[9] Both are recommended to be square in shape. It may be noted that the Brahmāṇḍa Purāṇa also prescribes that the square type is the best for a house.[10]

House-Building.

The Matsya Purāṇa goes on then to narrate the building of houses of four śālās, three śālās, two śālās, and one śālā. The catuśśāla or the four śālas, whether it be of a palace or temple, is known as *sarvatobhadra* and

6 Ch. 253, 2—10.

7 See I.H.Q., III, pp. 820—21.

8 *Ibid.*, Ch. 253, 47.

9 *Ibid.* 25—35.

10 Ch. 7, 108.

वृत्तं वज्रंचदीर्घं च नगरं न प्रशस्यते ।
चतुरस्रयुतं दिव्यं प्रशस्तं तै पुरंकृतम् ॥

considered auspicious. A slightly unsymmetrical building is known as *dhanyaka* or of three śālas. From this we are introduced to the building of royal mansions of which five kinds are distinguished according to their respective sizes. The best is the one with 108 hands in breadth by 135 hands in length. The four classes are each of them eight hands less respectively. Measurements are furnished as to the mansions of the Crown prince, Chief minister, other ministers, other officials and of the members of the four castes. It is said that the foundations should be invariably of well burnt bricks, as timber and mud are inferior and cannot stand the test of time. But it is interesting that this Purāṇa does not mention the use of mortar for building purposes.

Details are then furnished as regards the doors, joints, pillars of different sizes and measurements. What is of absorbing interest is that the Purāṇa states that paintings and carvings should be made in these pillars in the shape of a lotus, a creeper, a pot or a jar.[11] What we may call the artistic and human thought has come to influence the styles of architecture. The age of plain and simple art gave way to that of the decorative art which formed a principle feature of buildings. Wood carving and painting as fine arts had been introduced in much earlier times than we are apt to think. The Purāṇa recommends, we may note, a garden house and not a street house. For, says the Purāṇa, good and auspicious trees like the banian and the fig tree should be planted on all sides of the house.[12]

11 Ch. 255, 4.
12 Ibid., 20.

To a modern student of Indian art and architecture the planning of a house as detailed in the Purāṇa is of great value.[13] A dwelling house should not be built near a temple. There must be open space all round it. The trees are to be grown preferably at the back of the house. The site must be lovely and attractive. Flaws should be carefully avoided. If extension is made, it should be effected uniformly and symmetrically in all directions. The bathroom is to be located outside the main building. If these things are read together with the prescription of the Brahmāṇḍa Purāṇa where we have village planning and town planning with respective measurements for roads, streets, lanes, bylanes, they will go a long way to attest the development of architectural art in the early centuries of Christian era and perhaps much earlier.[14] The latter description agrees even in minute details with that of the Arthaśāstra of Kauṭalya and puzzles us to decide which is indebted to the other. Perhaps the version of the Brahmāṇḍa Purāṇa is older, and as I have said elsewhere, the Brahmāṇḍa Purāṇa is earlier than the Vāyu Purāṇa whose upper chronological limit can be fixed to be the 5th century B. C.[15]

Temple-Building.

The Purāṇa devotes three chapters to temple building.[16] He who is an expert in the art and science of housebuilding is recommended to fix up a site proper to

13 See Ch. 256.

14 Ch. 7, 105 ff.

15 See author's *Some Aspects of the Vāyu Purāṇa*, p. 46.

16 Chapters 268—70.

erecting the edifice of a temple. The usual prayers and offerings to the deity Vāstu are prescribed as a preliminary to the construction of any new building. Other deities like Rudra, Sūrya, are also to be propitiated. The site of the temple chosen was to be divided into 16 parts of which four parts were to be occupied by the *garbha* or centre. On all the four sides of the temples door-ways are to be made. Dimensions of the top, dome, passages for circumabulation and of walls are furnished, according to the plan of the temple determined upon. The different kinds of temples mentioned in the Purāṇa are:—

1. Meru with 100 tops (Śikhara) and 16 flats (bhūmika).
2. Mandara of 12 flats,
3. Kailāsa of 9 flats.
4. Kumbha of 9 flats.
5. Simha in the figure of a lion.
6. Mṛga with candraśālā.
7. and 8. Vimāna and Chandaka with several tops.
9. Caturaśra—square in shape.
10. Aṣṭāśra—octagonal.
11. Ṣoḍaśāśra—three flats and nice tops.
12. Vartula or maṇḍala—in the shape of a bull.
13. Sarvabhadraka or sarvatobhadraka, various tops and five flats.
14. Simhāsya—in the shape of a lion's face.
15. Nandana with several tops.

16. Nandivardhana—with 7 or 8 flats.
17. Haṁsā—resembling crane in form.
18. Vṛṣa one flat and round on all sides.
19. Suvarṇeśa—of seven or more flats.
20. Padmaka or pañcaka with 2 flats.
21. Samudgaka—16 corners ornamented with Pañcāṇḍakas.
22. Gaja—in the form of an elephant.

By far the most remarkable statement is that these different temples were built of bricks, wood or stone.[17] In the Valabhīcchandaka Gaṇeśa and Gaurī are also installed and this is considered auspicious.[18]

The Purāṇa then proceeds to give a categorical list of maṇḍapas or porches which always cover and precede the door leading to the cell. Of this twenty-seven kinds are mentioned.[19] The number of pillars generally determined the name of a maṇḍapa. For instance, a porch with 64 pillars is named *puṣpaka,* that with 40 pillars *yajñabhadra* and that with 12 pillars *subhadra*. The plan of these porches was triangular, square, circular, octogonal or with 16 sides. Three kinds of door—the best, the middling, and the inferior are also distinguished. The main gate was to be 140½ *aṅgulas* in height. On the west was a lotus pool of water, and on the east and south, were fruit and milky trees. In the south-east was the kitchen and in the north was the

17 Aiṣṭakāḥ dāravāścaiva śailā vā syuḥ satoranāḥ, Ch. 269—46.

18 Ibid. 54—56.

19 Ch. 270, 8 ff.

sacrificial chamber. In front of the Śiva shrine was located Nandi or Bull. There was also a place for the god Cupid. But this is not to be seen in the present day temples. Bells, flags and buntings were a speciality. The biggest maṇḍapa, according to the Purāṇa, was the porch with 64 pillars. In many of the temples today halls of 100 pillars and more are a redeeming feature and seem to be a later growth of Indian architecture. These halls are different from the porches and are used for common purposes. These point to the progress of art in India.

The Śikhara style.

It has been the opinion of archaeologists all along that the śikhara style of architecture with its curvilinear spire crowning the Hindu temples belonged to the medieval period of India's history.[20] In a note on a terracotta Rāmāyaṇa panel of the Gupta period Mr. K. P. Jayaswal has shown the existence of such a style of buildings in the Gupta period.[20a] The brick temples in this style belonging to the epoch of the Guptas are those of Deo Barnarak and Mahadeopur in the District of Shahbad in Bihar.[21] That the śikhara style is much more ancient is attested by the Matsya Purāṇa. Here are furnished varieties of the śikhara temples which go to prove the antiquity of the particular style of Hindu architecture. It is worthy of note that this śikhara style and Aṇḍa (Cupola) style have been framed after the model of the

20 See Codrington, *Ancient India*, p. 58—59.

20a See above pp. 47—48.

21 *Modern Review*, August 1932, p. 148—9.

mountain peaks and hills which are so named.[22] As if to corroborate this literary evidence the inscription of Kharavela[23] of Kalinga refers to the construction of lovely śikharas (varāṇi śikharāṇi)[24] another proof of the antiquity of the śikhara style of Hindu architecture.

The śikhara otherwise known as vimāna is in the form of a tower or spire intended to surmount the inner shrine or the *garbhagṛha.* The śikhara is in fact an external indication as to the location of the central shrine. A style of architecture corresponding to that furnished by the Black Pagoda at Kanarak in Orissa as given by Fergusson is referred to in the Mạtsya Purāṇa.[25] The tower is divided into 4 parts and the last two are the śukhanāsa.

This is the base. The third part above the base is the *vedika.* The upper part is surmounted by an *āmalaka,*[26] a massive circular stone supporting a vase called kapāla generally known as kalaśa. Perhaps kalaśa is the correct term. It is an old example 'as a sort of blocking course dividing the śikharas, horizon-

22 In a very interesting paper contributed to the *Bhandarkar commemoration* volume (1917), E. B. Havell contradicts rightly the theory of Fergusson that the śikhara temple is an indication of Dasyu extraction and traces it to Mesopotamian architecture of the second millenium B. C. where the Aryans are said to have ruled in Babylon for 600 years from about B. C. 1746. The curvilinear form, it is said, was derived from a similar watch tower built over the fighting car of the kṣatriya chiefs, the 'tank' of ancient Aryan warfare, (pp. 444—5).

23 2nd Cent B. C.

24 *Modern Review, ibid.*

25 Ch. 269, 18—19.

26 कण्ठमामलसारं तु ।

tally into numerous small compartments but curvilinear in shape.' In this case it can be asserted with confidence that the essential features of the design never changed.

It is even more remarkable that the Purāṇa mentions an ornamental arch of the temple of Viṣṇu on which were floral designs, images of vidyādhara, deva-dundubhi, Gandharva couples, lions and tigers, leaves and creepers.[27] This ornamental arch which the Purāṇa calls *toraṇa* is a chief feature of the Hindu temples, though it figures in some Buddhist monuments like the gateways of the stūpa at Sānchi. It is not known whether it was the horizontal arch or the southern style of Hindu architecture, or the horizontal dome its counterpart in the North on the same principle.

Brick as building material.

It would not be out of place here to examine the question when the use of brick and stone for architectural purposes came to be introduced in India. The late James Fergusson has remarked that 'it would be in vain to look for any earlier architecture of any importance in India before Aśoka's time: such could be expected only in countries where stone had been in use from the very earliest times.'[28] A critical examination of this statement leads to trace the chain of architectural evolution from rude beginnings. V. A. Smith marks three distinct periods of Indian architecture—the

27 Ch. 258—13.

28 *A History of Indian and Eastern Architecture*, Vol. I, p. 53. (1910).

'thatch period', 'brick period', and 'stone period'.[29] It can be readily conceded that the more primitive structures of the early Vedic and pre-Vedic epochs were framed in carpentry, and brick succeeded wood as the prevalent building material.[30] While it is admitted that the earlier temples like that at Aunda were built wholly in brick,[31] it is contended that the buildings of halls and temples as described in the Vedas and the Śatapatha Brāhmaṇa and later works belonged to the 'thatch period' in architecture. But this statement is open to many objections.

First comes the infallible testimony of archaeology. Recent excavations in the Indus valley have brought to light a number of interesting monuments which push back the history of ancient India to nearly an age coeval with the age of the Pyramids in ancient Egypt. This is not the place to examine in extenso all the details relating to the architecture in this period of Indian History. Suffice it to say that masonry of high order was established. The instances of the Great Bath,[32] and Pillared Hall[33] are sufficient. We have here the technique of brick laying[34] the manufacture of bricks[35] with the methods of laying, at different epochs, of varied dimensions and shapes, cut, sawn and marked. There is

29 *A History of Fine Art in India and Ceylon*, p. 23.

30 See Cousens, *Progr. Rep. A.S.W.I.*, 1894-5, p. 6.

31 *Ibid.*

32 Sir John Marshall, *mohenjo daro and the Indus civilisation*, pp. 15—17.

33 *Ibid.*, 160—3.

34 *Ibid.*, 271—80.

35 *Ibid.*, 266—8.

again a lavish use of burnt and sundried bricks. While the burnt varieties are used for such portions of buildings as are exposed to sun and rain, the sundried bricks are used for parts that are not so exposed.[36] Further explorations have brought to light massive buildings terraced and with stairways leading to upper storeys. According to the *Annual Report* (1928-29) a double staircase was found in a large and important building.[37]

The walls of houses relieved by ornamental recesses testify to the use of plaster on them.[38] What does all this show? The foregoing evidences point out that Indian architecture in brick was not post-Aśokan but it was as old as three thousand years at least before Aśoka. The message which these monuments have to impart to us is that we should revise though with caution, the prevalent notions together with chronological limitations we have been entertaining of Indian and Eastern Architecture. What is needed for determining the chronology of early periods is the stratigraphical evidence likely to be yielded by systematic explorations of ancient town sites not only in the North but also in South India.

Secondly there is the evidence of the Vedic literature itself on this point. Among the sacrificial rituals so elaborately narrated in the *Yajur Veda saṁhitā* there is the Garuḍacayana yajña where the sacrificial offerings are given on a garuḍa-like figure

36 *Ibid.*, p. 266.

37 See p. 71.

38 *Ibid.*, p. 18.

made of iṣṭaka or burnt bricks of varied measurements.[39]

Thirdly in the Sūtra period there is a reference to the gaming hall with a roof thrown over it. It is an edifice built by the king for the use of his subjects. One point of interest and value here is that the father is asked to make a hole in the roof of the hall to pull the boy through it. The rest of the details does not interest us for the present. The question of what this edifice was made and of what material the roof was made must engage our attention. Professor E. W. Hopkins thinks that the latter was made of thatch[40] assigning the reason that it can be easily repaired and that life depicted in the Sūtras is supposed to be country life. This supposition does not however stand in the light of unmistakable internal evidence. The sūtras of Āpastamba[40a] and Baudhāyana[41] imply the existence of towns. Again a public gambling hall would not and could not have been feature of every village. In those days it was more a royal amusement and the amusement of the citizens than of the rustic. It does not stand to reason that the roof was of thatch simply because it could be easily repaired. It could not be that kings who were responsible for such edifices used such flimsy and inflammable material for a public hall. Therefore it seems likely that brick if not stone architecture must have come into vogue much earlier than we imagine.

39 IV Kāṇḍa.

40 *C.H.I.*, I. p. 237.

40a II. 10. 25.

41 I, 32, 21 and II, 3, 6, 33.

Fourthly Megasthenes who visited India much earlier than the period of Aśoka refers to cities built of brick and mud. No doubt he like Strabo another Greek traveller, refers also to wooden buildings.[42] This does not mean that there were no brick structures. They existed side by side with wooden ones. In any age and in any country all could not afford to live in costly dwellings. Even today in many parts of South India we find a number of houses of earth side by side with well built stone houses. On this account we cannot say that we are still in the Vedic age. The evidence of Megasthenes then shows that the use of brick was known before the days of Aśoka.

Use of stone in architecture.

But the moot point in this discussion is to find out the existence of any tangible proof as to the use of stone in architecture. The use of stone depended more upon the region than anything else. Speaking of North Gūjarāt, Burgess[42a] has remarked that in regions where stone was abundant the brick stage may not have intervened. Though stone was not as easily accessible a material as brick, still its use for architectural purposes can be traced back to the third millenium B.C. and earlier as testified to us by the finds in Mohenjo-dāro and Hārappa. Apart from the rough stone structures we have tangible evidence of stone used in buildings[42b] in Sind which have been ascribed to the Stone age.[42c]

42 Indica, p. 68, (Maccrindle).

42a Vol. ix. A.S.W.I.

42b Marshall, *op. cit.*; p. 31.

42c *Ibid.*, pp. 92—3.

The restricted use of it is attributed to the fact that as stone of any kind does not occur in the alluvium of the Indus plain, it had to be imported from more or less distant places. That its use continued right on to historic times is corroborated by the following evidences.

First, Rhys Davids who has made a careful study of the Buddhist works and who generally writes with great caution has remarked that stone walls were a feature of fortification in India in the sixth century before the Christian era.[43] Speaking of the walls and remains of dwellings in the old city of Rājagṛha forsaken during the reign of King Bimbisāra, the contemporary of the Buddha to New Rājagṛha, the writer in the Cambridge History of India remarks that "such structures built of durable materials were certainly the rare exception rather than the rule in ancient India and were possibly essayed only in localities where stones suitable for such masonry were ready to hand."[44]

Secondly, the Kauṭalīya refers unmistakably to walls and other parts of building in stone. In fact in discussing the material for the passage of chariots, the Arthaśāstra insists on the use of broad and thick slabs of stones and condemns the use of wood, specifically assigning the reason that 'fire finds a happy abode in it.' This does not mean that Kauṭalya rigidly discarded the use of wood. There were

43 *Buddhist India*, p. 96.

44 Vol. 1, p. 616.

certainly wooden portions in the buildings. The Kauṭalīyan style of building is almost modern in character, and Kauṭalya, it may be noted, was the Chancellor Candragupta Maurya and his work therefore belongs to the fourth century B. C.[45]

Thirdly, there is again the evidence of the epic Rāmāyaṇa which testifies from the very nature of its description of the citadels of Ayodhyā and Laṅkā to an advanced state of civilisation with a similar advancement in social life. It cannot be maintained that the picture the epic portrays with all the architectural details full of grace and elegance is merely conjectural. Though it is difficult to assign a correct date for this work yet it is very much older in form than the other epic the Mahābhārata. From the description of the city of Ayodhyā in the opening chapters of the epic,[46] and on the eve of the prospective consecration of Rāma as Yuvarāja, with its lofty terraced buildings and halls inlaid with gems[47] it is impossible to reconcile oneself to the view that these edifices were entirely of wood and mud. Equally rich and, perhaps richer is the description of Laṅkā with its impenetrable fortress on the top of a lofty hill. There is an unmistakable reference to śilāgṛhas.[47a] There is again the significant reference to the fact that Hanumān who stationed himself on the toraṇa of Laṅkā citadel pulled down stones from it and threw them on the enemy

45 *See* Bk. II, Ch. 3 & 4. Also my *Mauryan Polity*, p. 333.

46 Rāmā: I, Ch. 5 & 6.

47 *Ibid*; II, Ch. 7 & 17.

47a V. 41. 19

below.[47b] The mention of golden pillars of sapta bhūmi and aṣṭabhūmi, of marble laid floorings, of windows with glimmer of pearls and diamonds,[48] all must point to the advanced stage of architecture unless it could be proved that the whole thing is false. Thus there are tangible evidences that go to prove the very early use of stone edifice in India, and in the light of such weighty testimony the theory of Fergusson falls to the ground.

Iconography.

Image worship: All national art is intimately connected with the religion of the nation. This was largely true of all ancient countries and in India it was the rule rather than an exception. In the Indus valley in the Chalcolithic age when the plastic art was past the primitive stage, we find clear traces of iconic and aniconic worship,[49] pointing to the antiquity of Śaivism and consequently Śaktism. The Indus valley people were iconolaters in the sense that they practised some kind of idolatry. Though there is no definite recommendation of the cult of idols either in the Vedic books or the earlier law treatises,[50] still idols came to be regarded as objects of veneration. With continued progress in art, religion came to be affected by a greater degree of encouragement being given to image worship.[51] In the Matsya Purāṇa as there is a great advance

47b V. Ch. 44, 9—16.

48 *Ibid*, V, Ch. 2.

49 Marshall—*op. cit.*, p. 58, 61.

50 C.H.I., p. 279, Vol. 1.

51 Sten Konow, *Indian Antiquary*, 1909, p. 145—9.

in the style of architecture, so also a similar advance is traced in the cult of idols and idol worship. In fact there is a definite and clear recommendation of this cult in several chapters.

In the Brahmāṇḍa Purāṇa we are told that to Paraśurāma engaged in penance Śiva appeared in the hunter's guise and Paraśurāma made an image similar to that form and continued his austerities when the Lord blessed him with his wish. In this connection a reference may be made to pl. cxvii, 16 of Marshall's *Mohenjodāro,* which figure we have tried to identify with Śiva as the Divine Hunter.[52] In this connection the Purāṇa theorises on the superiority of the Karma Yoga to Jñānayoga. One aspect of this Karma Yoga is said to be the installation of images of gods, worship of them by offerings and by holding festivals in their honour[53] thus showing that the Purāṇa is full of the idol cult.

Let us now turn our attention to the iconographic peculiarities of the pantheon as conceived in the Matsya Purāṇa. About ten chapters commencing with the Chapter 258 are devoted to details as to the making of images of various deities. The directions furnished may be favourably compared with similar details given in a later Purāṇa, the *Viṣṇudharmottara.*[54] The number of deities in the pantheon as conceived by the

52 See *Journal M. Uni.*, Jan. 1934.

53 Ch. 258, 1—8.

54 See Ch. 44—85 and also a summary of these in English by S. Karmisch—*Viṣṇudharmottara, Calcutta University*, 1928.

Matsya Purāṇa is too little in number if we can count the varieties in hundreds as actual sculptures demand our attention. A student of Indian iconography has to examine as his sources of information not only the literary material furnished in the Purāṇas and other literature on art but also the abundant sculptures in the host of temples scattered throughout this land to get at an idea of the evolution of art in ancient India. What we are concerned with here is the actual prescription of the Matsya Purāṇa in regard to the making of images of different gods. The first is that of Viṣṇu, an image with eight, four or two hands. A table of measurements is then enunciated. An household image should measure less than a cubit while that intended for a temple or palace can have a maximum height of 16 cubits. The thickness of several limbs is then furnished as pertaining to *navatāla* figures. While ten tālas (*daśatālas*) are assigned to the images of Rāma, Bali, Varāha and Narasimha, seven tālas (*śaptatālas*) constitute an image of Vāmana. No specific measurements are assigned to the images of Matsya and Kūrma which are perhaps left to the individual tastes.[65]

Then we have varieties of Śiva images—first as a youth of sixteen as if witnessing a dance, secondly as a dancer with ten arms wearing the hide of an elephant, thirdly a figure with 16 hands representing the burning of the three cities, fourthly of eight or four hands in the yogeśvara form, and fifthly of the Bhairava form. It

65 Ch. 259, 1—2.

is definitely prescribed that images like the Bhairava, Narasimha and Varāha are not fit to be installed in dwelling houses, and that any image with some defect in limbs will bring disaster and trouble to the worshipper.[56]

We have then prescriptions of the making of Ardhanārīśvara image,[57] of Śivanārāyaṇa, of Garuḍa, of Brahmā, of Kārtikeya of 12 hands with peacock for his vehicle, of Gaṇeśa with the trunk of an elephant, of Kātyāyanī, of Mahiṣāsuramardani, and of Indra and Indrāṇi.[58] Then there is a description of the making of the image of the sun,[59] the image of Yama with Citragupta, of the Lokapālas, like Varuṇa, Vāyu, Kubera, of Īśāna, and of mother Goddesses like Brāhmaṇī, Maheśvarī, Kaumārī, Vaiṣṇavī, Vārāhī, Yogeśvarī, of Lakṣmī, images of Kṣetrapālas and of Kāma.[60]

Then the Purāṇa narrates the pedestals of the different idols of which as many as ten varieties are distinguished. These are sthaṇḍila, vāpi, yakṣi, vedi, maṇḍala, vajra, padma, ardhasākṣi, and trikoṇa along with their general characteristics and measurements.[61]

The chapter that follows is on the installation of the *liṅgam* of Śiva in a temple and the prescriptions relating to it. It may be of ruby, diamond, crystal, clay and

56 Ch. 259.

57 Ch. 260, 1—20.

58 *Ibid.*

59 Ch. 261

60 *Ibid.*

61 Ch. 262.

wood.[62] Details as to the consecration of different idols at auspicious hours are furnished in Chapter 263 and in the succeeding chapter. Besides the offering and rituals, the accompaniment of music and dancing and Vedic chanting is insisted on.[63] A comparative study of the relevent chapters in the *Viṣṇudharmottara* shows a distinct advance in the evolution of art and in the popular practice of idolatry and iconolatry. We have images of moon, of the planets, of Vyoman, and Aiḍuka, of Manu, of Kaśyapa, of the earth, etc., which are not mentioned in the Matsya Purāṇa. Among the pantheon of this Purāṇa are the standing figures of Śiva with the different arms and in different postures. If we call to aid sculpture, there are few shrines today where we have Śiva in a standing posture and in those few again only four armed figures are to be seen. Rarely do we come across eight-armed figures. The Purāṇa is therefore much anterior to the date of origin of our present temples where the *liṅga* form has been universally adopted. This transformation must have been effected in the early centuries of the Christian era. It was again the period when Bali and Indra were worshipped as deities; while the first is scarcely known, the worship of Indra, an echo of which is seen in the *Indradhvaja* worship of later literature, is attested to by the Tamil classics, the *Maṇimekalai* and *Śilappadikāram* of the second century A.D. This points to an antiquity of Indra worship though it is difficult to trace its origin. Lastly the omission of the image of moon which is

62 *Ibid.*

63 Ch. 265—7.

again mentioned in the Tamil classics and in the *Viṣṇudharmottara* is significant. Though an examination of these sections does not lead up to decisive chronological limits, it is still of value as throwing welcome light on an aspect of Indian culture which has been much neglected and whose importance cannot be sufficiently recognised.

CHAPTER V.

ITS INDEBTEDNESS TO THE VĀYU PURĀṆA.

In the tangled skein of ancient Indian chronology it is difficult to assign definite dates for particular compositions. It is assumed here that the Vāyu Purāṇa is much older than the Matsya Purāṇa. Looked at in any way, the Vāyu Purāṇa seems to contain much older material than we are apt to credit it with. If one may so put it, the Vāyu Purāṇa belongs to the epoch of the earlier form of Yoga, a characteristic feature of the early school of Śaivism. This theory has been corroborated by the recent finds in the Indus valley which have been assigned to the Chalcolithic period. Of this practice of yoga, there is nothing in evidence in the Matsya Purāṇa. On the other hand it is a treatise that lays stress on the Karma aspect of the Hindu religion. But it must be noted that there is no conflict between Karma and Yoga. As conceived by the ancient Hindus, Yoga is a phase of Karma. While the former is a mental action, the latter is a physical kriyā, rituals and ceremonials constituting Karma proper. If this position is granted, it logically follows that this aspect of Karma is a later introduction that came in after the fire cult assumed prominence. It was realised perhaps that the difficult practice of yoga could be the monopoly only of a few and could not by any means be a practice of the masses in general. Hence elaborate rituals were made incumbent on the individual members of the Hindu community as a whole. In this section it is not our purpose to discuss the thought and religion of the Matsya Purāṇa. A study of the two purāṇas shows that the Vāyu Purāṇa is a much earlier composition from the point of view both of its matter and of form. Viewed in this light the passages occurring in the Matsya Purāṇa which are closely parallel to those of the Vāyu Purāṇa must be taken as a copy of the latter, with slight modifications in the names of persons or places. As most of these names are not quite intelligible to the ordinary reader, one has to remark that even in copying passages verbatim, the copyist has gone wrong, sometimes to such a great extent that it would be impossible of proper identification and interpretation without a comparative study of the companion volume, the Vāyu Purāṇa.

The copying of the Vāyu Purāṇa by the Matsya Purāṇa is indeed a systematic one. It is not a copy of a few lines here or a few stanzas there, taken from the Purāṇa at random. It is on the other hand an incorporation of a whole chapter or chapters as the case may be.

The verse[1]

Eṣṭavyāh bahavah putrāh yadyekopi gayām vrajet|
Gaurīm cāpyudvahetkanyām nīlam vā vṛṣamutsṛjet||

1 Matsya P. Ch. 22, 6 and repeated in a slightly altered form in Chapter 207. 40, and the Vāyu P., Ch. 105. 10.

is common to both the Purāṇas and seems to be a later addition in the Vāyu Purāṇa, from the Matsya Purāṇa where it looks more appropriate. In some of the manuscripts of the Vāyu Purāṇa again this is not found.

The chapters (113) and (114) of the Matsya Purāṇa entitled Dvīpādivarṇaṇam and bhuvanakōśa seem to be bodily taken from the Vāyu Purāṇa: Chapters 34, st. 2-57, ch. 43, st. 1-9, ch. 45, st. 2-20, ch. 45, st. 69-137, ch. 46, st. 1-37. The system of copying is, as has been already said, far from satisfactory. Some stanzas are left out while a few, though very few, are added. And these additions again do not appear very relevant. Again the chapters (121 to 128) entitled Jambūdvīpavarṇanam, dvīpavarṇanam, sapta-dvīpa varṇanam, candra sūrya bhuvana vistāram, sūrya candrāmaścāram, sūryādigamanam, dhruvapraśamsā and devagrahavarṇanam, closely follow the Vāyu texts. The relevant chapters in the Vāyu Purāṇa are 47, st. 1-80, ch. 49, st. 74-103, 106-7, 182; ch. 50, 56-224, ch. 51, st. 2-76; ch. 52, st. 1-71; ch. 52, st. 71-99, ch. 53. st. 2-121.

The following few among a host of examples will demonstrate how the words are mutilated and corrupted in the Purāṇa and in some cases entirely new words are substituted.

Matsya.		Vāyu.	
Maṇidhara	121—13	Maṇivara	47—12
Varuṇa	—19	Aruṇa	—17
Nalini	—55	Pāvini	—53
Vamśankasāra	61	Vasvokasāya	60
Mṛgyā[2]	—69	Jyotsnā	68
Madhvī	71	Mādhvī	71
Jambūdvīpa	122—2	Krauñjadvīpa	49—75
Gatabhayam	—21	Jaladam	—85
Munitapta	—30	Anutaptā	—91
Veṇuka	33	Dhenuka	94.

The chapters again (141-145) śrāddhānukīrtanam, manvantarānukalpa, devarṣisamvāda, yugavartanam and manvantarakalpavarṇanam, under the common division of manvantarānukīrtanam closely follow the Vāyu Purāṇa, ch. 56:1-94; ch. 57, st. 1-125; ch. 58, st. 1-125; ch. 59. 3-105.

The chapters 271-272 entitled Rājavamśānukīrtanam, and ch. 273 entitled bhaviṣyarājanukīrtanam are again the Vāyu texts reproduced with a few alterations. The corresponding portions in that Purāṇa occupy st. 281—365 of the chapter 99. This means a portion of the lengthy chapter in the Vāyu Purāṇa dealing with the dynasties of the Kali age is furnished in three chapters in the Matsya Purāṇa.

From the titles of chapters which correspond with the Vāyu version as given above one has to infer that the author of the Matsya Purāṇa in point of the cosmogony and geography, astronomy and astrology, and the

2 Another reading is Vitastā.

details relating to manvantaras and the dynasties of the Kali age found the Vāyu text a safe guide to follow in the main particulars.[3] If chapters 113 and 114, 121—8, 141—145 and 271—3 which number altogether seventeen, and which closely follow the Vāyu texts may be eschewed from the Matsya Purāṇa, then the original of the Matsya text consisted of 274 chapters only, though there are passages common to both this Purāṇa and the Padma Purāṇa. It is a moot question to decide whether, the Padma Purāṇa is earlier than the Matsya Purāṇa, or the other way about. Orthodox tradition is unanimous in crediting the Matsya Purāṇa with much more importance and trustworthiness than the Padma Purāna. In fact the concluding verse of this Purāṇa runs thus:[4]

Purāṇam sarvaśāstrāṇām yadetanmūrdhni saṃsthitam

This does not seem to be mere self-glorification. Its greatness and value as well as antiquity have been unanimously recognised by Indian literary tradition. If this tradition can be credited the Matsya Purāṇa must be regarded much more ancient than the Padma Purāṇa.

3 See Author's *Some Aspects of the Vāyu Purāṇa* (Madras University, 1933), where a brief enumeration of the above topics has been made.

4 Ch. 290—25.

CHAPTER VI.

THE TAMIL MATSYA PURĀṆA.

Curiously enough there is a world of difference between the printed editions of the Matsya Purāṇa, (See for instance Poona edition) and that of the Tamil version of the *Macca Purāṇam.*[1] This means that the author of the Tamil Macca Purāṇam had before him a manuscript or manuscripts of the Matsya Purāṇa which was different from that or those on which the extant Sanskrit editions are based. It is not possible to say what manuscript this Tamil author consulted and followed, where he got it and whether there is still a possibility of getting it. As I have said elsewhere, the ancient Tamils were acquainted with some of the important Purāṇas so early as the beginnings of the Christian era.[2] That the *Viṣṇu* and the *Liṅga Purāṇās* were known is indicated by the evidence and the authenticity of the twin epics—Śilappadikāram and Maṇimekalai. The *Macca Purāṇam,* tradition attributes, to a certin ruling chieftain of

1 The *Macca Purāṇam* published in Madras (1900) with an Introduction in Tamil by Mr. S. Anavaratavinayakam Pillai, M.A. The Purāṇa is translated in verse which is elegant and simple. From an inscription 365 of 1912 recording a gift of land and a house in the Devadāna village Sorappūṇḍi to Pandit Vaḍamalaiyar of Arruvanpāḍi, Prof. V. Rangachari thinks that this Vaḍamalaiyar was probably the Tamil poet who wrote the Maccapurāṇa and Niḍurttalapurāṇa. If this identification be accepted the date of the author must be fixed somewhere in the first half of the 16th century. The record is dated Ś. 1446 corresponding to 1523. (See *Inscriptions of Madras Presidency,* Vol I, p. 50).

2 *Indian Historical Quarterly,* Calcutta, *The Purāṇas—A Study—* (Dec. 1932, pp. 765—67.)

Tinnevelly by name Vaḍamalai Appa piḷḷaiyan who flourished in the middle of the sixteenth century A.D. The work contains 5000 stanzas. The Purāṇa is divided broadly into two parts—the Pūrvakāṇḍam, containing 3015 stanzas and 114 chapters, and the Uttarakāṇḍam containing 1986 stanzas and 58 chapters. The first three chapters are prefatory to the main work of which the third *anukkirāmaṇi* contains a table of contents.

Taking up then the *pūrvakāṇḍa* for a comparison with the Sanskrit Matsya Purāṇa we find that the Tamil work consists of 114 chapters, while the same portion is spread over 160 chapters in the original treatise. The following differences may be noticed.

(1) In the chapter (16), the verses 16 and 17 of the original are not found in the Tamil work. The verses in question relate as to who are to be discarded for purposes of Śrāddha rituals.

(2) In chapter 18 of the Tamil Purāṇa which deals with the sapiṇḍīkaraṇa ceremony and cases of pollution there are certain additional stanzas which are not traceable in the original (see for example, p. 74, st. 6 ff. p. 76, st. 25 ff).

(3) In Chapter 34 entitled 'the anointing of Pūru' of the Tamil Purāṇa, one again notices additional details not to be seen in the Sanskrit original. (See for example, p. 114, st. 6 ff., p. 116, st. 18—22, p. 117, st. 30 ff, p. 118, st. 36 and 37; p. 119, st. 45 to the end of the chapter).

(4) In chapter (35) of the same work entitled 'the attainment of Heaven by Yayāti', on p. 121, stanzas 10—15 are again additional matter that have no corresponding passages in the Sanskrit original.

(5) Again in chapter (39) of the Tamil Purāṇa, on p. 129, the stanzas 9 and 12 are additions.

(6) Up to chapter 44, we find no difference in the titles of chapters which closely follow the original. Chapters 45 and 46 of the Matsya original are treated under one chapter (45) in the Tamil translation. Again chapter 48 of the original is split into two chapters in the translation as 49 and 50. But in the chapter (50) of the Tamil work, chapter (49) of the original commences with stanza 19 and thus the end of the chapter (50) of the Tamil Purāṇa is the close of chapter 49 of the original. This disparity in the arrangement of chapters goes on to the end of chapter 61 of the Translation, corresponding to chapter 60 of the original. Chapter (65) of the Matsya Purāṇa "akṣayyatṛtiyāvratam" is left out in the Tamil translation. Going further we find the chapters 81 and 82 of the Sanskrit original entitled Viśokadvādaśīvratam have been compressed into a single chapter (81) of the translation.

(7) In chapter 47 of the Tamil version, the stanzas 57 to 60 furnish a brief summary of the original legend in which Bṛhaspati assumed the guise of Śukrācārya and persuaded the asuras from accepting the leadership of Śukra.

(8) The Matsya Purāṇa devotes chapters 83 to 92 to an examination of the ten kinds of gifts, which

are all treated in more or less a summary fashion in a single long chapter (82) of the translation. One can easily mark out these ten chapters of the original in this eighty-second chapter, and it is interesting to note that the spirit of the original is not in the least sacrificed. Towards the close of the chapter 10 verses of the original are left out in the translation.

(9) We see again that chapter 93 of the original forms chapter 83 of the translation. This chapter cannot be said to literally follow the original. For while the original has 161 verses, the translation contains only 73 stanzas, thus demonstrating that an abridgement of the original is alone attempted in it.

(10) The chapters 84 to 88 correspond to the original 94—98. The matter of the two chapters of the original 99 and 100 is treated in a single chapter of 89 in the translation. And the chapter 90 corresponds to chapter 101 of the Matsya Purāṇa. This correspondence is continuous up to chapter 109 of the original which agrees with 98 of the translation.

(11) The chapter 99 entitled in the Tamil book 'anointing of Dharmaputra' furnishes the matter scattered in the original in the chapters 110—112.

(12) Again the chapters 100 and 101 of the Tamil book contain the matter of chapter 113 of the original. The chapter 102 of the translation is in correspondence with the original 114. One notices strict adherence to the original until the 109th chapter of the translation which equates with chapter 121 of the Matsya Purāṇa.

(13) The chapter 110 of the Tamil book corresponds to chapters 122—3 of the original, chapter 111 to chapters 124—5 and chapters 112—4 to chapters 126—8 of the Matsya Purāṇa. With this ends the Pūrva Kāṇḍa of the Translation.

(14) The Uttarakāṇḍam begins with chapter 115 and does not, like the Pūrva Kāṇḍa, follow the printed edition of the Sanskrit Matsya Purāṇa. This Kāṇḍa opens with an account of the penance of Hiraṇyakaśipu and contains the story of his entry into his royal hall of audience. Devas' deputation to Viṣṇu and narration of his evil deeds, Viṣṇu's assurance of support, the legend of Prahlāda, the incarnation of Narasimha, death of the asura, anointing of Prahlāda are all related in detail in a number of chapters followed by a few chapters dealing with the science of yoga, bhakti, etc. These constitute the first thirty chapters of the translation, and strenuous search in the original Matsya shows that it contains a bare skeleton of the legend of Narasimha slaying Hiraṇyakaśipu and that is found chiefly in two chapters 161 and 162. It would appear therefore that the translator worked upon an entirely different manuscript which is perhaps lost to us.

(15) It is curious to note that chapters 31 to the end (ch. 58) of the translation deal primarily with the matter scattered in the chapters 129 to 160 of the Poona edition of the Matsya Purāṇa. Though it cannot be said to follow the original in the literal sense, yet there is demonstrable evidence that the spirit of the matter is not affected in the least. We can therefore conclude

that the Tamil translator continues the thread as furnished by the Matsya Purāṇa. A re-arrangement of the chapters in the Tamil version of the Uttarakāṇḍa will prove the truth of this statement. If the Uttarakāṇḍam commences with the thirtieth chapter and if chapters 1—29 are arranged after the present 59th chapter, one will notice that it forms a continuous account.

Even then the Tamil Purāṇa is incomplete. The total number of chapters of the Matsya Purāṇa are 291 and the Tamil translation, even in the order we suggest for the re-arrangement, will end with chapter 162, and thus nearly 130 chapters constituting more than 1|3 of the original are found omitted in the Tamil translation. This critical analysis seems to give an indication that the original on which the poet-prince Vaḍamalai-Appan worked was at the best an imperfect copy or to venture a conjecture, was the available southern recension of the 16th century A.D. If the manuscript bore that peculiar classification of chapters, it is worth our while to institute an earnest search for that manuscript which may throw fresh light on the Matsya texts in general.

INDEX

ERRATA.

P. 78, l. 15, *for* intellegentia *read* intelligentsia.

P. 107, l. 24, *for* principle *read* principal.

P. 122, l. 20, *for* śaptatālas *read* saptatālas.